Karate Doesn't Work in a Phone Box

From Bruce Lee to Brazilian Jiu-jitsu:
A Martial Arts Journey and Other
Life Lessons

Gary Savage

Published by Scaredy Cat Publishing

© 2020 Gary Savage

The author asserts their moral right to be identified as the author of this book.

First published in Great Britain in 2020
by Scaredy Cat Publishing.

ISBN 978-0-9935718-3-1

All rights reserved. No part of this book may be reproduced in any written, electronic, recording, or photocopying without written permission of the publisher or authors, except as permitted by the UK Copyright, Designs and Patents Act 1988, without the prior permission of the publisher.

Although every precaution has been taken to verify the accuracy of the information contained herein, the author and publisher assume no responsibility for any errors or omissions. No liability is assumed for damages that may result from the use of information contained within.

This book is sold subject to the condition that it shall not, by way of trade or otherwise, be lent, resold, hired out, or otherwise circulated without the publisher's prior consent in any form of binding or cover other than that in which it is published and without a similar condition including this condition being imposed on the subsequent publisher.

Cover design by Danny Rich
Cover photograph by Jason Savage
Interior photographs by Ian Charlton
Edited by Paul Robinson

enquiries@scaredycatpublishing.co.uk

I first met Gary in 2005 back to the greatest Wolfslair Gym in Widnes where I was the head coach. Later in 2005 we started a partnership; Gary became my student and I started teaching classes once a week at his gym in Blackpool.

In 2011, before returning to Brazil, I had the honour and pleasure of graduating him as a Black Belt. In December of 2014 Gary went to Brazil to improve his Jiu-Jitsu and to visit me. At the time he made me the proposal to return to England. Thanks to him, today I have my own gym in Liverpool and our team is stronger than ever.

Gary is a true friend, an excellent Jiu-Jitsu coach and a wonderful human being. Thank you, Gary, for your friendship and loyalty.

"To the regiment...I wish I was there."

- Mario 'Sukata' Neto
  5th Degree Black Belt in Brazilian Jiu-Jitsu
  Black Belt in Judo

Dedication

This book is dedicated to a man that gave more than he took, listened more than he spoke and was loved more than he knew. My Dad, my Hero, my greatest teacher, Bill Savage

And to the strongest woman I have ever met. For whom the poem *Invictus* may well have been composed, Grace Savage.

Whenever I want to see you, I just close my eyes as Jim Reeves sings your song, "Welcome to My World", and there you are.

The Nightmare

I am standing at a crossroads.

I look forward, but a thick fog impairs my vision. I see a shadow moving towards me. It is now taking form. The breath leaving its body, bleeding into the denseness of the already misty air. Its eyes are cutting, laser-like through the fog; red, angry and soulless.

I can now make out a shape. A grotesque and disfigured body, with hands outstretched to claws yellow and razor sharp, its legs pumping powerfully to carry the demon towards its prey. And then it is in front of me. Its putrid breath warming my face. The demon raises its hand, balled into a fist and arching towards me. Instinct sees my hands go up in defence, but the force of the blow is too great, and I am sent reeling back, landing heavily on the cold tarmac.

I scramble to my feet. I look down each road that forks away from me, but I see nothing. The hairs on the back of my neck stand as I feel the warm air of the demon's breath, I turn but it's too late. The beast grabs my throat, lifting me effortlessly into the air. I struggle to break its grip, but I can't. I look into the eyes of my foe, and ask, "What do you want with me?"'

"I want your future," replied the cackling, shrill voice.

Field of Dreams

"If we build it, they will come."

The United Kingdom has long enjoyed a heady love affair with the Martial Arts. Decades before the Bruce Lee craze of the 1970's, the British public had been introduced to the benefits of Karate and Judo as both a self-defence and alternative sporting pursuit. From our capital city to the Home Counties, sports centres and draughty village halls have long echoed to the sound of hand slapping mat and the, "Kiai!" war cries from an ever-growing legion of British martial arts enthusiasts. These pioneer British practitioners of Judo and Karate worked tirelessly to build a strong foundation, both visiting, and later bringing over their Japanese masters to teach the authentic training and techniques of their respective arts. Since these halcyon days, we have embraced the many variant martial styles that have wended their way from their homeland and onto this green and pleasant land.

It is no surprise that Great Britain has turned out to be such a welcoming foster home for all things Martial. For centuries the British have stood shoulder to shoulder in battle. Fighting, it is said, is in the blood of the inhabitants of this land. For such a small island, we have a rich history of violence. Not content with defending our country from pillaging and hostile invaders, our armies have, in turn, crossed continents in their quest to gain a foothold and strengthen the might of the British Empire.

Aside from our fighting prowess on the battlefield, the British are credited with being the founding fathers of some of the most effective hand to hand combat systems known to man. Pugilistic bare-knuckle contests gained popularity as early as the 16th century in England. These bloody and barbaric encounters, known as fisticuffs, were fought with scant regard for human life or safety. Rules were later introduced to popularise the sport amongst all classes and with the introduction of timed rounds and 'mufflers' (an early boxing glove prototype), the sport evolved into the art that is now referred to as boxing.

Although the British are readily acknowledged for their development of boxing as an unarmed combat system, we receive less credit for our wrestling prowess. In fact, the British Isles were, in times past, a stronghold for many variant grappling arts (some of which are still practiced in mainland Britain).

In the mill and mining communities found in the North of England, wrestling flourished for a time. Wrestling offered the locals a reprise from the often-harsh living and working conditions that were common to the day. The most prolific style of wrestling practiced at this time was Catch as Catch Can, (Catch Wrestling) which incorporated throws, joint locks and pins within its arsenal.

The Northern town of Wigan became an epicentre for the art of Catch Wrestling. The infamous Snake Pit Gym, as it was later to be known, was home to a Catch Wrestling legend called Billy Riley. From the 1950's on, Riley's Wigan-based sweatbox had a hard and fearsome reputation for turning out some of the best and most accomplished wrestlers of the day. The harsh training environment and gruelling regime forged the skills of a group of wrestlers that would go on to win major titles across Europe and America. Karl Charles Istaz (known better by his ring name, Karl Gotch) was one of the Riley Gym standouts.

Although born in Belgium, Gotch grew up in Germany where he began his formal wrestling training. It wasn't, however, until he made the decision to move to England in order to train under Riley that his skill level rocketed, and he subsequently started to enjoy success on the international competition circuit. Karl Gotch readily embraced the rigours of the daily wrestling workouts imposed by Riley, but he started to look further afield to enhance his already immense strength, stamina and physique.

Gotch took further inspiration from training and watching the Indian wrestling systems such as Pehlwari. He incorporated Hindu push-ups and squats into his daily routine, regularly completing a thousand reps in each daily. Under the tutelage of Riley, Gotch became Catch Wrestling's most famous ambassador, later fighting and living in Japan where he was affectionately known as "The God of Catch Wrestling."

The golden era for Catch wrestling in Great Britain sadly didn't last and, with its popularity waning over time, it morphed into the pantomime and much 'worked' spectacles aired on British TV screens of the 1970's and 80's. (Today, Catch Wrestling is enjoying something of a revival, and the traditions of the old masters are being passed down to a new generation of eager students, which hopefully will ensure that British wrestling's authentic heritage is restored and celebrated).

Chasing the Dragon

The 1970's heralded the start of a golden age for the British Martial arts scene. Not only was this a time of great prosperity for the already established martial arts schools, but it was also the era of a martial gold rush that saw hundreds of new instructors staking their claims and cashing in. The main catalyst for this sudden explosion of interest in the fighting arts was Bruce Lee.

Lee had shot to fame in the UK in 1973 following the release of his fourth film, "Enter the Dragon". Ironically, Lee was already dead by the time his Martial Arts Masterpiece blazed across Western silver screens. His early demise only added to the mystery that surrounded him and created his enduring legend.

Before Bruce Lee, the Martial Arts were very much an underground movement in the UK. Lee introduced the benefits and beauty of Kung Fu to the masses, and as a result, gave a kick start (no pun intended) to all Oriental fighting arts. It was the striking-based systems that mainly profited from the Kung Fu craze that swept Britain in the 70's. With Karate schools enjoying record numbers of new student enrolment everyone, it seemed, wanted to mimic their hero and become a high-kicking fighting machine. Wily Chinese immigrants saw an opportunity to teach their 'real Kung Fu' to the eager masses, and soon it felt like there was a Martial Arts school on every street corner in every town and city across the country. Bruce Lee's legacy and influence survived long after the initial furore of 'Kung Fu Mania' had died down, and for a time, the traditional Martial Arts systems continued to flourish. Bruce Lee's influence had unwittingly opened a floodgate that made Great Britain a true multi-cultural Martial Arts haven.

Having No Style as Style

The 1980's witnessed something of a Martial Arts revolution. Some hardcore Bruce Lee fans had started to look towards Lee's theories of real combat and, in particular, his penchant for cross training and blending systems in order to be effective in all areas of combat.

The perceived rigidness of the traditional Martial Arts was suddenly so last season amongst the enlightened few. The traditional Martial Artists derided cross training as a fad, insisting that it offered little in the way of substance or depth. In turn, the cross-training fraternity criticised the traditional arts for purporting myths, and worse, of duping their students into believing that the ancient techniques they taught were *street effective*.

These new-breed practitioners shunned many of the traditional elements of the Martial Arts. Many stopped (if they ever started) wearing the traditional uniforms (Gi). They followed the mantra that belts were only good for holding up the trousers and didn't see any benefit in marching up and down the dojo, punching and kicking thin air in robotic unison.

The cross-training fraternity practiced Western boxing alongside kickboxing and incorporated grappling and takedowns to their arsenal of techniques. They followed the teachings of Bruce Lee the Martial Artist, not Bruce Lee the movie star. Lee's own interpretation of Martial Arts was called Jeet Kune Do, *the way of the intercepting fist*.

Lee had discovered, through empirical research, that his base style of Wing Chun was practical in some areas but lacking in others. He believed that the traditional styles were too entrenched in their classical teachings. They hadn't moved with the times or adapted to the 21st Century. Lee wanted to strip his fighting style down to the absolute minimum, not be constrained by a set of ancient doctrines passed down from some long-deceased figure head. He saw his art as ever evolving, a free-thinking and uninhibited liberal expression of the human body.

The legacy that Lee left is more than that of the action hero he portrayed on the silver screen. He offered a new perspective on combat, and importantly, brought systems that had previously been separated by continent and culture, together. This was a healthy time for the British Martial Arts scene and gave rise to a host of home-grown talent, many of whom would go on to leave their own mark on Martial Arts history.

The Boys from Brazil

If the 1970's were the era of the high-kicking arts, and the 80's the cross training years, then the 1990's can be celebrated as the era that brought Brazilian Jiu-Jitsu (BJJ) to the British Isles, and although there might be some debate as to who the first Brazilian Jiu-Jitsu teacher in the UK was, there can be little argument as to why BJJ found a place in our martial history.

In 1993, the Martial Arts world was rocked to its core following the inaugural Ultimate Fighting Championship (UFC). The competition pitted style vs style in a bid to answer an age-old question- what is the most effective unarmed combat system in the world? At the end of the no-rules contest, a young Brazilian called Royce Gracie's arm was raised and it seemed that the question was answered. Gracie's stature in the Martial Arts Hall of Fame was assured when he repeated his achievement at UFC 2 and 3. The martial art that prevailed for Royce Gracie was Jiu-Jitsu. He was the smallest competitor at UFC 1 and looked the least-likely to survive, let alone win.

Royce Gracie was victorious despite his perceived disadvantages. The win cemented not only Royce's place in martial arts history, but also introduced his families' art, Gracie Jiu-Jitsu to a whole new audience. UFC 1 made the world wake up to the fact that some of the arts that we considered 'deadly' were, in fact, lacking in terms of their practical applications. The Gracie style of Jiu-Jitsu was unlike anything most practicing martial artists had seen before. In fact, the thought of someone fighting *off their back* was abhorrent to most traditional martial artists, who for years had never even considered a ground fighting scenario.

For many, UFC 1 was purely an entertaining spectacle. For others it was a defining moment in their lives. The birth of Mixed Martial Arts was imminent and with it, a shift in perception as to what 'real' combat should look like.

Brazilian Jiu-Jitsu entered the Royal Court as a fresh prince, with its eye firmly on the Martial Arts crown. Although Gracie Jiu-Jitsu may have seemed like a brand-new art, it had its roots buried deep and firmly planted in the past.

Brothers in Arms

Helio, and his older brother Carlos Gracie, are credited as the founding fathers of modern-day Brazilian Jiu-Jitsu. Over 70 years ago the Gracie family (a Brazilian family of Scottish descent) had refined the techniques that had been taught to them by a Japanese immigrant called Maeda.

Maeda, also known in Brazil as the 'Count of Combat' was a Judoka and prize-fighter who had previously toured the world, spreading his art like a latter-day Martial Arts evangelist, before permanently moving to Brazil as part of the early 19th century settlement agreement between the two countries. Maeda had taken Carlos Gracie as a student and, in turn, Carlos had shared his new-found knowledge and skills with his brothers, before setting up his own school, the first Gracie Jiu-Jitsu Academy.

The techniques that Maeda taught the Gracie brothers came from Kodokan Judo and the self-defence applications that are found in traditional Jujitsu. The Gracie brothers initially taught the moves as intended, but later Helio, the youngest and reportedly weakest of the brothers, developed his own variations of the techniques in a bid to make them more practical to someone of his size, build and physical limitations. Helio worked out that by using leverage, the moves were considerably more efficient regardless of the size or strength advantage of an opponent. It was Helio's theory of leverage that was to form the basis of the Gracie Jiu-Jitsu blueprint, and ultimately distinguish it from Judo and traditional Jujitsu or, for that matter, any other Martial Art.

Not content with pure theorizing, the Gracie family set out to prove their arts' effectiveness in a series of challenge matches that were destined to make the family famous in their native Brazil, and later around the world. The challenge, or 'Gracie Challenge' as it became known, was posted in a Rio newspaper advert. Carlos Gracie had worded it:

If you want your face punched and bruised, your butt kicked, and your arms broken, talk to Carlos Gracie at the following address...

Not subtle, even by today's standards, but the advert worked perfectly, and soon the challengers were queuing up, to prove their fighting prowess against that of the Gracie family Jiu-Jitsu.

Helio Gracie stepped up to face this initial onslaught of challengers. Exponents from Capoeira (the Brazilian Martial Art), Karate, Judo and Western boxing were amongst those that tried, but failed, to impose their will against the Gracie style of Jiu-Jitsu. Helio and his brothers gained national fame from their victories, and as a result their Jiu-Jitsu became the toast of 1920's Rio high society.

The Gracie Challenge set Jiu-Jitsu apart from other combat systems. It dared to challenge outside of its own confines, where boxers fought other boxers, and Karate and Judo faced their own practitioners under their own specific rule sets. The Gracie Challenge opened up the world of combat, to make it style vs style competition. It trained a microscope on itself and other systems in order that it might show up any weaknesses within its arsenal of techniques. It was the epitome of an art whose main quest was continual improvement and evolution. The UFC was the natural progression for Gracie Jiu-Jitsu to continue in its quest to prove that it was the world's most complete fighting system. Rorian, (Helio's eldest son) used the UFC vehicle to propel his family's art from home-grown fame to worldwide fame overnight.

Rorian, a law graduate, came up with the premise of the show to highlight his belief that Gracie Jiu-Jitsu was superior to any of the other hand to hand combat systems that were popular at the time. Of course, Rorian already had his Father and uncles' experience from the Gracie Challenge as a baseline from which to start. Royce Gracie was chosen as the Gracie representative, not because he was the best fighter, but because he was the opposite in looks and physique to the archetypal image of a fighter. Softly spoken, his face unmarked by previous combat, Royce was considered the perfect advertisement for Gracie Jiu-Jitsu. And on that November night in Denver, Colorado, he didn't disappoint.

The UFC 1 card was stacked with Martial Artists from a variety of backgrounds. Royce was the lightest competitor (There were no weight limits or rounds at UFC1) that night. He entered the octagon in style, in a human train comprising of his Father, brothers, uncles and cousins, later to be called the Gracie Train. Easily dispatching his first opponent, Royce moved into the next round unscathed, everything was going to plan for the *Brazilian First Family* of Jiu-Jitsu. In fact, Royce made short work of all his opponents at UFC1. Using his takedown to mount or other control position, before applying his finish if the opponent didn't tap-out before the submission was applied. Most of the other competitors were like fish out of water once their initial punches or kicks were thwarted by Royce. It became evident that the majority had never been on the floor as part of their Martial Arts or previous combat experience. Even the commentators at UFC1, all experienced Martial Artists, showed a lack of understanding as to the Gracie game plan. Royce being held aloft by his brother Rickson remains a fitting and iconic conclusion to UFC1, but if those watching the tournament thought that it was a fluke or indeed a fix, their scepticism was dealt a further blow in the next UFC instalment when Royce, fresh from spending his previous pay cheque in Disneyland, repeated his UFC 1 performance in devastating fashion. This time the doubters had to sit up and take notice.

The Gracie name was quickly established, and the baying fans had a new hero in Royce Gracie. Royce's victory at UFC 1 and 2 made him both saviour and destroyer of Martial Arts. He destroyed the myths that some fighting arts were unbeatable and that the exponents of these arts had mystical powers, but he also showed that his style of combat was real and that you didn't need to look like a comic book hero to be effective. Maybe there was no death touch reality at UFC 1 and 2, but there was definitely a previously unseen power at play, and it was accessible to all. Gracie Jiu-Jitsu had arrived. UFC1 was not only the catalyst for launching Gracie Jiu-Jitsu onto the World stage, but it also notably led to the birth of Mixed Martial Arts (MMA) as we now know it. Following Royce Gracie's success at the first and second UFC events, the future competitors started to study the ground fighting techniques that previous Martial Artists had been found to be lacking in. It was also around this time that Wrestlers started to look towards the UFC as a potential way of using their base art to make some money. The Wrestlers studied striking and with their ability to not only impose their will to take an opponent to the mat, but also keep a fight standing, they soon became a force to be reckoned with.

For the Gracie family, their success at the first UFC tournaments proved that their art was the most effective Martial Art, but with the rise of the Mixed Martial Artist their time as Kings of the Octagon were numbered. The evolution of the sport saw the future stars of MMA training all areas of combat equally, and the very best had no weaknesses in their game. They were as comfortable standing as on the ground.

The UFC had raised the consciousness of a new generation of Martial Artists. Jiu-Jitsu academies flourished, and people started to see the benefits of studying the art for both its self-defence and sporting applications. Outside of Brazil, the USA became an epicentre for the art, with many Brazilians setting up academies and riding the crest of the wave of interest created by the UFC. Gracie Jiu-Jitsu soon became known colloquially as Brazilian Jiu-Jitsu and while the Americans enjoyed their privileged place as Jiu-Jitsu's second home, the rest of the world waited.

For UK fans, BJJ was to prove to be somewhat elusive. Some of the early British pioneers travelled to America to study the art, returning to our shores the proud wearers of the coveted Blue Belt. To the rest of the small band of brothers patiently waiting, the thought of attaining a Blue Belt was almost an impossible dream, but a dream that we refused to give up on

BJJ was out there. We knew that, if we were patient, it would come to the United Kingdom just like the Japanese and Chinese Martial Arts had in the past.

I was one of the dreamers.

1

A Boy Named Sue (nearly)

"There is always one moment in childhood when the door opens and lets the future in." Graham Greene

1963. Four mop topped Scousers were causing teenage girls across the globe to hyperventilate. Dr Martin Luther King, an American Civil Rights activist, made his "I have a dream" speech, and Lee Harvey Oswald assassinated John F. Kennedy in Dallas, Texas.

Elsewhere, on a cold November morning in that very same year, in news that was ignored by the tabloid press (how rude), I was born.

The birth, like most things that were to follow in my life, wasn't exactly a walk in the park. I refused to give up without a fight, and after a gruelling labour, the Doctor decided that the only way I was coming out was by forceps delivery. For those that don't know, this procedure involved my head being clamped by what could easily be mistaken for a pair of pliers, and the Doctor pulling me out, much like a dentist extracting a bad tooth.

Bloody, and obviously not in the best of moods, I was plonked onto my Mother's lap. I'm sure she wasn't exactly ready to jump for joy either, as I proceeded to scream the hospital down in an act of pure contempt for this unfair end to what had started out as a fair fight.

I was what old ladies might describe as a *bonny baby*. In short, I had a head like a watermelon and was chubby with it. The forceps delivery had probably not helped with the unusual head, but the bulk was all down to the fact that I was a greedy little bugger.

As was the custom in days gone by, my Dad was tasked with choosing a name. A name that traditionally should be bestowed on a son and heir and therefore synonymous with virtues such as strength, courage and honour. Quite a responsibility and no easy task. Dad went away to think it over. And think it over and, well you get the gist, he wasn't going to be rushed. My mother waited with baited-breath, the family waited. Hell, even I waited.

When at last he appeared, much like Moses bringing down the Ten Commandments from Mount Sinai, he said proudly and with a straight-face, "Tracey. I want to call him Tracey."

Can you imagine going through school, first job, and later entering the minefield that is dating, saddled with a name like Tracey? This book may well have taken a different course. I think I might have ended up a serial killer had he stuck to his guns. Either that or Johnny Cash might have written a song about me. Anyway, good sense prevailed, and they eventually settled on Gary James.

I was the second born. My Brother, Ray, had arrived with little fuss a couple of years earlier and, luckily for him, my Dad hadn't felt the need to give him a girl's name. I settled into a life that only those coming in a close second will relate to. I graduated from being a hand-me-down baby, to a hand-me-down kid. Clothes, shoes, toys - you name it - I got it second-hand. I also quickly realised that whenever my brother got into trouble, I somehow ended up sharing the blame. A sort of secondary blame. The one thing that we got at the same time was our dodgy haircuts. My Mum used to put a pudding bowl over our heads and go to town like a demented Edward Scissorhands. So, there I was, not yet into double figures, with holes in my pants, shoes that were too big and a haircut that obviously later inspired Lloyd in the film "Dumb and Dumber".

Lock up your daughters!

2

When You're Young

"Our lives were just beginning, our favourite moment was right now, our favourite songs were unwritten." Rob Sheffield

From Woodstock and The Beatles' last live performance, to a man walking on the moon, the decade known as *the Swinging Sixties* ends in style. And the hopes and aspirations of a generation are to be severely tested as we welcome in the new decade.

My Martial Arts odyssey began in the 1970's, after I got caught up in the Bruce Lee craze that, along with Chopper Bikes, flared trousers, platform shoes, Glam Rock and thankfully later, the arrival of Punk Rock music, helped to define my generation.

The 1970's in Great Britain were a particularly unsettled time that saw the decade split between the two main political parties. This was the era of power cuts, where industry was ruled by the unions and the ever-constant threat of 'one out, all out' strikes. It was also a time of innocence, where we blindly believed that Gary Glitter's only crime was the dodgy wig and stage wear (not to mention Rolf Harris and his didgeridoo). We lived through the Winter of Discontent and sweltered through a summer drought. Life wasn't all bad. It could have been a lot worse with the gift of hindsight; my letter to 'Jim'll Fix it' might have got picked.

My reality was typical of any working-class family. Living on the outskirts of Liverpool, and struggling to make sense of the real world, I didn't have time for worrying about the economy, or anything else for that matter. This was a time of adventure, a time when we *played out,* regardless of the weather, when computers were only hinted at in science fiction movies and the closest thing we had to a mobile phone was walking to the telephone box at the end of our road.

It wasn't all sweetness and light for kids born into the 60's and growing up in the 70's. Parenting was stricter, and we were ruled with a rod of iron. Not for us back chatting or demanding things that would leave the family short of money. A popular phrase of the day being, "children should be seen and not heard". In other words (excuse the pun), we had no voice. At Christmas and birthdays my presents were often made in my Dad's workshop. One year he gave me a wooden fortress made of plywood to house the plastic soldiers I collected religiously. It was one of the best presents ever. Money couldn't buy a gift like that. It came from the heart and took imagination and effort.

Sometimes, if my parents had extra cash from either Mum winning at the bingo or Dad's overtime, we got a bike or a skateboard to keep us from feeling left out of whatever craze was presently sweeping the country. My brother, ever the wit, got to one of my presents before me one Christmas. He went to a lot of trouble removing the wrapping paper and the Action Man from the box, before re-wrapping and leaving a note saying that this was the latest in the line-up of Action Man figures, 'The Action Man Deserter'. Christmas that morning started with a brawl and probably ended the same way. But we were always thankful, whatever we got, be it a home-made toy or a Chopper bike. Had we dared to complain, the present would be bagged up and given to someone who would appreciate it, or at least threatened (it never actually came to that). The same with the food on our plates. If we left something, we got the lecture about starving Africans, how we were lucky to be British, and the most affluent of nations.

We lived in a modest semi-detached house that had been greatly-improved by my Dad's DIY skills. My parent's marriage, at least on paper, shouldn't have worked. My Mum, Grace, was a Londoner of Romany Gypsy stock, never shy to tell people how she was feeling, and my Dad, William (Billy), was a quiet Yorkshire man who, after serving his country, had enjoyed a brief time as a professional cyclist.

They had met when Dad was competing in the Tour of Britain. The team had rested up at a holiday camp where my Mum had been taking part in a beauty pageant, and the rest, as they say, is history. To my Mum's horror, Dad's dream honeymoon saw them on a bicycle made for two, touring the long and winding roads of Ireland. He rarely drank and was as straight as a dye, so my Mum's cigarette and bingo lifestyle often saw them fighting like cat and dog. But even though at times they were close to killing each other, woe betide anyone that dared to come between them.

Holidays for us were always in the United Kingdom, and I never went on an aeroplane until I was well into my 20's. Aeroplanes and foreign travel were only seen in the James Bond movies that I and most of the UK population in the 1970's loved to watch (with only 3 TV channels there wasn't much choice). We considered ourselves lucky if we went camping in Wales, trekking up mountains like Snowdon, or fishing in rivers until the sun was replaced by a star-filled sky. The holidays in Wales, although fun, always ended the same way. Mum would be cursing the ignorance of the local people whom she insisted would start talking in their Welsh dialect whenever an English person entered a shop or pub ("ignorant bleeders", her words not mine).

Inevitably, the car would break down on the way home. Whatever, we always seemed to go back to the same places year in and year out, if we had the spare money. One of my early memories comes from a trip to a river near Snowdon. Our kid (my big Brother) wanted to go fishing for trout, and Mum had asked my Dad to make sure I was clean for the journey home (in those days I loved mud). His decision to wash me by dipping my semi-naked body into the river nearly saw my life cut very short (I was about 6 years old). Dad lost the grip he had on me, and I recall bobbing about in the water. Going under, time and again, the outside world replaced by a blue/green uncertainty that was both frightening and yet strangely calming. I heard my Mother's screams mixed with the whooshing of rapidly-moving water as it carried me to a certain watery grave. In that moment, my life went into a slow-motion sequence. I felt the water coursing into my mouth, filling my lungs, taking my life. And then, the reassurance of another land-dweller.

Dad had dived in and pulled me back to the surface. I gasped for air. The sky above an umbrella of hope, something familiar. I felt myself hauled through the air before landing heavily onto the grass that bordered the stream. Dad clambered out next to me. Mum was crying, as was my brother Ray, although he was more pissed off that the fishing had been disturbed than by my near accidental drowning. I, too numb to realise how close I had come to shaking hands with the Grim Reaper, lay shrouded by sharp green blades of grass. The journey home, I was later told, saw my Dad, sodden to the skin and driving for two hours in his underwear. As for me, I slept on the back seat, knowing that I had been lucky to have a Dad that could swim and, more importantly, willing to put his own life at risk to preserve mine.

These annual holidays were great, an escape if you will, but once home and back to so-called normality, a cold feeling would envelope me. I don't recall when it started or when I changed, or maybe I didn't, and it was always inside me. A blackness, that over the years I have come to know so well. Hand in hand with some very dark and desperate thoughts that I struggled to understand, was a feeling that I never quite belonged. I was what people might now describe as *uncomfortable in my own skin*.

School was especially difficult; I just didn't get it. Sometimes described as quiet and at other times a human tornado, disruptive and unruly. I hated the regimentation and found the "3 R's" (reading, (w)riting and (a)rithmetic) difficult (see what I mean). I made some friends, but often sought solitude away from the numbers. At home I had a special hiding place under the stairs, a tiny dark space where no one could see me, and here I could while away the hours, lost in a daydream, stepping out of myself and into an imaginary world. A world where I was happy, free and able to cope. I started to study the other kids at school, noticing how they acted. And, although I was very introverted most of the time, I started to take on their personas, or at least the traits I admired; their sense of humour, the cockiness in front of the teachers, even down to copying their walks and mannerisms. I didn't realise it, but I was inventing a public persona in order to fit in. A persona which once alone I could shed like a skin. I was a chameleon long before I knew what a chameleon was.

Children can be cruel, especially if they think you are different. I now see that my personality change was a coping strategy, a way of deflecting attention. I was terrified that the mask would slip, and people would be able to see the real me. Whatever, or whoever that was. I remember our first colour TV. I felt embarrassed to tell my mates about it, afraid of being called middle-class or, worse still, posh. There was no worse label, not that there was much chance of anyone believing we were either.

My Dad had been left some money following the death of his parents. It must have been a good amount because not only did we get the colour 'telly', but Dad also got a new car - a Maxi that I recall was sprayed gold. Before the inheritance we, like most of the families we knew, got new stuff on the 'never never', (so called because no matter how long you seemed to pay, you never got to the point of being out of the original debt), catalogues, or from shops that did 'tick' (buy now, pay later).

Both the television and the car were my parent's pride and joy. They were the first things of material value that they had bought outright. That car was polished to within an inch of its metal work and the TV was always having the colour sliders adjusted to get the best possible picture. Dad seemed to have a second sight, because he could see shadows on the figures on the screen that no one else could. And usually it was during a favourite programme of mine, like The Saint or Randall & Hopkirk Deceased, that he would rise from his favourite chair to take the back off the box and fiddle with the inner workings. In Randall & Hopkirk's case, my protestation that it was about a ghost and that's why there were shadows, often fell on deaf ears. Either that, or he just didn't like Randall & Hopkirk. Rarely did the mysterious shadow appear in a John Wayne cowboy film.

The TV was a fine gadget, it was cased in a cabinet that when the doors were closed looked like any other piece of mahogany furniture. I think this was an attempt to fool any burglars that might pay us a visit. We also had that most working-class of rooms in our house, the Parlour. This was my Mum's pride and joy, a kind of Nirvana where the pressures of the time or, for that matter, dust molecules ceased to exist. We were never allowed in the parlour, it was a mythical place that was all chintz, lamps and cushions. It smelled differently to the rest of the house, all shag-pile carpet and wicker furniture. Occasionally the parlour would be used, but only on special occasions such as a visit from posh people (not that we knew many). Not only did the house change during these most-honoured visits, but strangely so too did my Mum's usual London accent. It went from Cockney to Royal Family in a second. Something I noticed again when later we acquired our first telephone, a slim, trill model that was always answered in the same way. The telephone number would be recited back to the caller as if to make sure they had got the right person, followed by my Mum's best impression of the Queen, asking, "Can I help you?" My brother Ray and I were never allowed to use the phone, and God forbid if one of us got to it first, we found ourselves hauled off by the scruff of the neck by my Mum who had sprinted faster than Speedy Gonzales to get to it before we could open our common mouths.

3

We Don't Need No Education

"I have never let my schooling interfere with my education." Mark Twain

School was different back then.

The teachers were not afraid to use any means necessary to control the class, be it belt buckle, hand or cane. Our primary school headmaster, Mr Anderson, was a surly gentleman with a cold, hard face that looked like it had been chiselled from granite. His eyes were blank, rarely giving away any emotion or feeling. Tall, at least that's how I remember him, he had a strange smell that I now realise was a mixture of cheap cologne and the pipe that he puffed on between lessons. He looked, to me, like a Russian (or what I imagined a Russian would look like, again thanks to James Bond). Walking around the playground in a fur hat and large overcoat, rarely smiling or addressing the children other than to tell some unfortunate how useless they were.

The 1960's state education system was run like a conveyor belt, churning working class kids through curriculums that were, in the main, aimed at producing the foot soldiers that society needs to keep the top 5% in their privileged positions. Following graduation, those that were motivated joined their parents on the factory floors or, if they weren't totally beaten down by the system, an apprenticeship in one of the trades. Someone must go *over the top*, and you can be sure it wouldn't be the old school tie wearing Etonians and titled few. Anderson was certainly no Miss Jean Brodie, and he and others like him were nothing short of card-carrying thieves that stole the dreams and aspirations of the young minds with which they had been entrusted and tasked with broadening.

Mum had an almighty row with Anderson one day after she discovered my brother was behind with his reading. She called Anderson all the names under the sun and threatened to remove us from the school, and worse, Anderson from his faux-Russian headpiece (not to mention where she was going to shove his pipe). Anderson may have been an imposing figure to an 8-year-old but, faced with this 5-foot 3-inch Cockney firebrand, he shook like a shitting dog and apologised profusely.

Mum was always the one with the temper. Size or reputation never phased her. I remember her many times marching around the estate to confront someone's parents if she thought that their precious offspring had wronged my Brother or me (usually we had got in over our heads). She always dragged us behind her on what seemed like the longest walk to the perpetrator's house and made us watch her giving the bully a good going over. And not only the bully, but the parent as well, if they were stupid enough to stand up to her. Mum's actions made us kids feel untouchable, and soon we built a reputation as a family not to be messed with.

My brother Ray mirrored my Mum's side of the family when it came to gambling, even at an early age. I took after her with my quick temper, the perfect combination in my brother's eyes. Too young for the bookies or bingo, my brother would make his money betting on playground fights, or whatever else would turn an easy profit. He was like a mini Don King, minus the hairstyle and gold jewellery. I was the obvious choice for the main card of these early *No Holds Barred* challenges. Usually the odds were stacked against me, as the kids I was to do battle with were my brothers age, and as a result two or three years my senior. But that didn't stop him (or me). I went along with his plans because I liked to fight, and I believed in his *family honour* pep talks (he must have watched The Godfather for inspiration).

These fights seemed to follow an unwritten ritual. There was the pushing and cajoling for position, and the goading from the spectators, who would then form a tight circle around the combatants and chant 'fight, fight, fight'. One or both would then start spitting, occasionally puncturing the silence with the word, "Yeah?"

These routines could go on for several minutes, or until one of the fighters, pressured by the heckling and baying crowd, would throw a punch, or go for that most-common of schoolboy techniques, the headlock. If caught in a headlock, you were often spun around until you landed on the spit-wet ground, your opponent squeezing for all they were worth, whilst asking desperately, "Give in?" I was proud of my headlock. I knew that nine times out of ten it was a winning move. Occasionally, from the headlock the best transition was to sit atop your fallen foe and rain down some punches (early *ground and pound* style). The sight of blood was usually enough to stop a fight, with the more sensitive and fair-minded in the crowd pulling the entangled and flailing combatants apart. A forced handshake would follow, and the two boys would head off home for their tea.

As we got older, the fair play seemed to fade. Kicks were aimed at downed opponents and the onus was on how much you could mess up the other lad's face. The threats of getting your "head kicked-in" started to be banded around the playground, as kids vied to be the 'cock' of the school.

My reward for fighting, along with the black eyes and bloody nose, was a good hammering from my Mum when I got home. My Dad would wait until Mum was out of earshot and ask the result of the fight with a glint in his eye. I loved that; it gave us a bond. Ray was never suspected as the Mr Big of the underground fight club that he was running. He was the original mini Teflon Don (King), nothing could stick to him. Always the Angel in my Mother's eyes, whereas I was the problem child, a social hand grenade. If she had thought about it, she might have seen that we were more alike than anyone.

Things were about to change in me. Maybe it was the violence, maybe it was the things that I felt were out of my control. Either way, I was struggling to fit in, not only with my friends, but my family too. I felt like an outsider. I just seemed, suddenly, capable of the vilest actions and behaviours. Children see things in black and white, without the wisdom of time or experience. For me, I felt at best to be misunderstood, and at worst, unloved. I morphed into a twisted and angry child, incapable of emotion, or at least emotion that could be seen from the outside. I am ashamed to say that I became a bully, a nightmare, a mixed-up child, angry at everyone and everything. I lashed out at strangers because I was incapable of dealing with the reality of my situation. I woke angry and went to bed the same way. The once-righteous young soul was burnt to charcoal by the overwhelming hatred of anyone that tried to get close to me.

Back in the day, we knew little of mental illness. When I was quiet, I was told to *snap out of my moods*. When elated and overly enthusiastic, I was told to *calm down*. The only constant was the raised voices and angry reactions of adults.

I started stealing. The odd fiver here and there from Dad's wallet, and the odd cigarette from Mum. I started giving treats to my mates like I was loaded. I felt like the big man. Anyone that I didn't like, or suspected as weak, I tortured. I once tied a kid to a lamp post and beat him until he was near to losing consciousness. Blood covered my knuckles, his cries echoed around my head, but I didn't care. His pain couldn't match mine. His bruising would fade. I cared little for him or his suffering. As far as I was concerned, he was a casualty of war. A war that I was losing every day. To me, this lad was in the wrong place at the wrong time. Inconsequential, unimportant, a loser in the race of life. Cars were stopping and adults shouting for me to stop the brutal attack, and yet it didn't deter me. The Police became regulars at my door. I had a lucky escape after I hit an older kid over the head with the iron rod that held our drive gates together. His head had split like an over-ripe tomato, but I still chased him and gave him some more. He was so afraid afterwards, that he refused to name me as the attacker, but everyone, including my parents, knew it was me.

I was now asking my brother to get me fights. The beatings masked the real hurt that I was experiencing, giving me respite at least for a while. But, once alone in my bed, I was again the lone benefactor to a world of inner turmoil and pain. My brother noticed the change. For a start he knew I smoked. His reaction saved me from a lifetime of nicotine addiction when, one day, he lured me to the canal. I would have followed him to the ends of the Earth and he knew it. When we got to the cut (the Leeds Liverpool Canal), he asked me if I could see the millions of minnows that were swimming just below surface. As I got onto my knees, head just above the water, he struck. My head was pushed into the smelly, cloudy water that played host to a thousand discarded prams, condoms and shit that nobody wanted or needed anymore. I struggled but, overcome by the surprise of the attack and the stench of the canal, I was out of my depth, literally. As I gasped for breath, I felt a hard kick to my ribs and a series of well-aimed punches to the back of my head. Groggy, both from the rancid water in my lungs and the attack, I was finally hauled out and onto the pathway. My torment wasn't to end just yet. My ever-resourceful and loving brother produced, for my delight, a pack of twenty.

"Smoke," he shouted, the anger apparent in his contorted face.

"Come on, Dickhead. Have a fag."

He made me smoke the full pack, one after the other, until I puked into the already-filthy cut, green and putrid, the final resting place of life's unwanted shit. Guess what, I never smoked again (thanks bro).

My brother always really had my back, despite some of these stories painting him as a bit of a rogue. He is one of the most decent human beings I have ever met and I'm proud to call him brother.

Anyway, I was a shit thief and eventually my Dad found out. His punishment wasn't to beat me - that I would have welcomed. It was to be much worse. He sat me down and told me how disappointed he was, and, in fact, he was ashamed of me. I would gladly have taken a beating. To him, ex-army, straight as a dye, never a bad word to say about anyone, I had lived up to my Mum's view of me, something he had always argued against.

I wanted to curl up and die, right there.

4

Everybody Was Kung Fu Fighting

"It is like a finger pointing away to the moon. Don't concentrate on the finger or you will miss all the heavenly glory." Bruce Lee

July 20th, 1973. Before the vast population of the planet knew who he was, Lee Jun Fan, or as he became universally known, Bruce Lee, died. His death gave life to the rumours and mystique that endure to this day. And, much like other Hollywood stars or musicians that die before they fulfil their potential, the legend was destined to overtake the reality.

People often say that they can remember exactly where they were and what they were doing when they hear news that defines its place in history, such as the day JFK was assassinated, Elvis dying, or the moment Neil Armstrong had his 'one small step for man' moment. Well I can recall, in glorious technicolour, the day that I heard about Bruce Lee's death, even if I had no clue who he was at the time.

I had started at the local Cub Scouts. My parents had figured that it might keep me out of trouble, at least for a while. I had just arrived at the scout hut, when a boy called Dave came running up to our small group of eager *dib dib dibber's* shouting, "The King of Kung Fu is dead." I must admit, the words didn't really mean a lot to me at the time, but something about the following conversation caught my imagination.

"David Carradine?" I asked.

"No, Bruce Lee, you Dickhead!" replied Dave.

Not very nice language from a member of Baden Powell's finest. I don't recall there being a profanity badge to go next to your basic knots and first aid badges.

"Who?"

I genuinely had never heard of this 'Bruce Lee'.

"Bruce Lee. He's the real king of Kung Fu. He's been killed by Chinese gangsters, or something," continued Dave, revelling in his story now, and not allowing the truth to get in the way of a good yarn. "Yeah, he was the fittest man in the world. He could kill someone with one kick."

Okay, I was listening.

"He was the fastest puncher ever, he learned in a Shaolin Temple, just like Kwai Chang Caine, but real," Dave continued.

Ah, now I understood. I loved the Saturday night TV series *Kung Fu*. The story of a wandering monk that could kick the crap out of ten baddies without breaking a sweat.

That night at Cubs proved to be memorable for another reason. It was the night that I was asked to leave by the troop leader. It should have been my proudest moment, the night I was awarded the prize for bringing in the most charity money from 'bob a job' week. A week of helping the community, by knocking on doors offering to do small jobs for money.

Nothing wrong in that, no problem so far. I had proudly handed over my 'takings' and felt the rush of excitement mixed with a tinge of pride. I imagined myself being cheered and carried around the room by my fellow toggle-wearing comrades in arms, but, alas, it wasn't to be.

The leader of the troop, Akala, or whatever she called herself (I think her real name was Edna) had other ideas.

It appeared that the local neighbourhood (my neighbourhood) had been terrorized by a gang demanding money for shoddy or non-existent work. And worse, I was named as the gang leader. My brother had a few of his mates helping, for a cut in the profits, but I genuinely was shocked to be branded 'a gang leader, preying on the local community'.

Talk about stifling the talent of a future entrepreneur. If not for this unfortunate episode, I might have gone on to become the next Lord Sugar, or at least his apprentice.

Not my finest hour. I still recall the shame, well, that was the word my Mum used when telling my Dad all about it when he got home from work. So, along with my discovery of Bruce Lee, I now needed a new focus. I didn't really want to be remembered as the kid that was kicked out of the Cubs. I wanted to learn more about this dead Kung Fu star. My imagination was running wild, and I wanted to know what all the fuss was about.

I didn't have long to wait. One day, when I was off school with a cold, or some other life-threatening virus that pre-teens acquire to get out of double maths, my Mum arrived home with a magazine for me. This magazine was the first ever 'Kung Fu Monthly'. It was dedicated to Bruce Lee and, as a bonus, once you had read all the content, it opened out into a huge poster of the man himself.

This was the first time I had seen a picture of the mysterious 'King of Kung Fu'. If cool had an image, then this must surely be it. I couldn't think about anything else, other than being like Bruce Lee, who I had still only seen on the cover of a magazine. I was yet to see the man in action. I just knew from the poise and grace of his pictures that he would not be a disappointment when I eventually got to see a Bruce Lee film. But that day was a long way off, and in those days the movies were all X-certificates, meaning that I had more chance of seeing Lord Lucan riding Shergar down our road than of seeing a Bruce Lee film.

I was desperate to learn this exciting new fighting style. It didn't matter to me whether it was Chinese or Japanese, I wanted to be like Bruce. I hounded my Dad to teach me some of the moves he had taught in the army, but he was selective in what he would show a ten-year-old ex-Cub, local gang leader who seemed to attract trouble without even trying. The stuff he did impart was great. I loved those early days. He taught me some rudimentary Boxing and what I now realise was some wrist locks and throws from an Aikido and Jiu-Jitsu base. We often had play fights, which always ended up the same way. Me on the floor, with Dad's carpet slipper across my throat, tapping-out to the patented wrist lock. Along with the play fights, we would also have some interesting talks where I would quiz him about all things fighting. One such conversation went something like this:

"Dad, is it fair to scratch and bite in a fight?"

"Yes, if you're losing," chimed in my older brother.

Dad agreed, saying, "In a life and death struggle, it is anything goes."

I was a bit taken aback. In my 10-year-old view, biting and scratching was a girl thing. I asked my Dad if he had ever had to do these things, to which he replied, "Only when I killed Adolf Hitler, son."

Wow. To this ten-year old's ears, this was amazing. I knew he had basically won the war single-handedly, but doing Hitler in with his bare hands? Now, that was a big thing.

"Did you use karate, Dad?"

"No, we were taught unarmed combat. Karate moves are okay, but they don't help you in a confined space."

"What's a confined space, Dad?"

He pondered on my question.

"Karate doesn't work in a phone box, does it? There's no room for all that flowery stuff. In unarmed combat you learn to use what's available, and to adapt to your situation."

"So, did you kill Hitler in a phone box, Dad?"

The question hung in the air, never to be answered, but it didn't matter. Dad's revelation kept me quiet for the rest of the day. I didn't quite understand what he meant, but it kind of made sense. Long before Bruce Lee, this five-foot three Yorkshire man was my Hero. It never occurred to me to question his many stories. I mean, of course, it made sense that he had climbed Mount Everest, or his claim that the James Bond stories were loosely based on his days with the Secret Service. So, the image of Hitler being garrotted in a phone box with the receiver wire filled me with pride. I couldn't wait to tell my mates.

Play fighting and talking about fighting gave my Dad and I a special bond, I always believed that. I relished our time together and wished I could have had the same bond with my Mum, but that wasn't to be.

I didn't go looking for fights (most of the time), they just seemed to happen. But the sight of me striding proudly down the drive with blood dripping from my nose or a nice shiner really didn't help my plea to join a Martial Arts class. Eventually my Mum capitulated to my constant whining, after someone told her that the discipline would do me good.

She enrolled me at the local Karate school, an offshoot of the Red Triangle Shotokan club that was famed across the UK at the time. At last, I was going to learn to kick someone in the head, like Bruce Lee.

I didn't have a Gi. My Dad was hedging his bets after shelling-out on the wasted Cub uniform that now hung (shamefully) in the downstairs cloak room - a sad and constant reminder of my Kray Twins bob-a-job escapade. I suppose Dad wanted to see how long the Karate club would put up with me before he entered into yet another potentially bad investment.

He needn't have worried, I loved it from the first moment I entered the Dojo, feeling like I had finally found a place that I felt comfortable in. It was handy because the Karate club was just around the corner from my Mum's favourite bingo hall, which meant I got to go three times a week, and it wasn't long until the old man gave in, and I got my first Karate suit (Mum had had a biggish win at the bingo).

I would happily practice my punches and kicks up and down the training hall in search of perfection, and when home I practiced some more. I wanted to be as good as the Sensei, Steve Cattle. He may not have looked like a typical Karate hero, being bespectacled and sporting a comb-over that reached past his shoulders when he was in full flow, but his technique was flawless. His punches had snap, and his kicks, crackled and popped. He was quite a scary person, especially to a 12-year-old. Even if he did resemble a bank manager.

The training was hard. It wasn't uncommon for the entire class to be jogging around the streets in barefoot unison or doing push-ups on our knuckles before the technique and sparring.

I was the youngest member of the squad and was, in the main, looked after by the adults. I loved the sparring, especially if I was paired with Steve Cattle, but however much I tried to land a roundhouse or reverse punch on him, I never got close. His instep would playfully slap my head and his punches were pulled as he showed me who was boss.

The more I trained, the easier I found the more complex techniques and Katas. I was totally immersed in the Karate lifestyle. But, no matter how much I loved the training, and looked forward to it as the highlight of my week, I never got away from that feeling of fear every time I walked into the training hall. It was a bit like the feeling you get when walking into a Hospital - the smell of disinfectant invoking a horrible heaviness in the pit of your stomach, right up there with that first day at a new school or being the newbie at your first job. The fear of the unknown.

No matter, I always got past the uneasy feelings and, as soon as class started, the feeling was replaced by an utter happiness and a sense of belonging. Occasionally there would be new starters. Some stayed, most didn't. They soon found that the training regime, and Sensei Cattle's no-nonsense approach, was not for them. I liked it when people dropped out; it kind of reinforced my thinking that this was only for a chosen few. Those that were tough enough to get through the endless sit-ups, push-ups and the hard knocks given in sparring. Don't get me wrong, Steve Cattle terrified me, and if I was under his watchful eye, I was a total jelly.

But, if I thought Sensei Cattle was scary, I was soon to have my eyes opened by the man they called 'The Tiger'.

Sensei Enoeda (The Tiger) came to visit our school to give a seminar. This man was a God to the Shotokan Karate fraternity. The seminar must have been expensive because I recall my Dad groaning when I told him the cost.

Dad wasn't too trusting of the Japanese either, finding it hard to forget their role in WW2, but he paid the exorbitant fee anyway. I was over the moon at the prospect of training under a real Karate master. For weeks leading up to the course, I was a ball of energy, practicing at every opportunity. I dreamed that Enoeda would think I was a prodigy, worthy of becoming his student. Perhaps he would take me to Japan where I would be his full-time apprentice? I would spend my days cleaning the Dojo and train three or four times a day, slowly becoming an unbeatable Karate Ka, my body a chiselled weapon that would rival Bruce Lee's.

I saw myself as something of an English Ninja. I would learn to walk on rice paper without leaving a footprint, demolish bricks with the flick of my hand, be able to jump backwards and land gracefully on a tree branch - you get the picture. After many years of hard training, I would return to Blighty, and Sensei Cattle would be the one hitting fresh air as I danced effortlessly out of reach, before closing the distance and up-rooting him with a solid side kick. He would sit, despondent, his comb-over spiralling to his knees, head in hands, and look up at his once weak student who could now say, without doubt, that he had indeed become the Master.

Dreams are great, but at some point, the alarm goes off and reality hits you like a cold shower. And boy, was I about to get a wake-up call.

My enthusiasm was swiftly curbed by Enoeda's teaching method. His English was very poor, and he barked instructions that I just couldn't understand. He also carried a stick that he would use on the legs and stomach of any student that he felt was not quite grasping the technique.

I was terrified of messing up in front of him, but that seemed to make me worse. I suddenly forgot my left from my right and was soon on the receiving end of his stick and his bad English. At the end of the day I was just relieved to get out alive. I told my Dad it was great, even though I was disappointed in myself, and still a little shaken from my first encounter with a bona fide Japanese Master. And to top it off, it looked like Sensei Enoeda would pass on me being his full-time student.

Just as well really, as I didn't have a passport.

5

The Times They Are a Changin'

"I am extraordinarily patient, provided I get my own way in the end." Margaret Thatcher

Eventually, I made it to the grade of Purple Belt in Shotokan Karate. But, at 13 years old, my Martial Arts bubble was about to burst.

As the country sang along to the Grease soundtrack, Liverpool's once-flourishing industry was sinking and the working-class heroes, that turned in day in and day out to put the 'Great' in Great Britain, were fighting just to keep it afloat. The unions were battling for fair pay and the whole country, or maybe just the part I knew, seemed to be on strike.

It was the first time I had heard the term Black Leg. According to my Dad these black legs were traitors to the working-class movement. Their sin - to cross the picket lines and work, thus betraying the cause. The very line that my Dad, and many like him, turned out to defend. Striking was the only way that the worker had any leverage against the fat cat bosses.

It wasn't all about money. Some of the industries were making people redundant and replacing the discarded worker with cheap or unskilled labour. But, if we thought we had it bad in 1978, we had reckoned without Margaret Thatcher.

In 1979, the Conservative Party came to power and Britain had its first female Prime Minister. Thatcher revelled in her nickname, 'The Iron Lady'. Her bouffant, heavily-lacquered hair, dark blue suits and well-rehearsed cut-glass voice became the epitome of evil to the downtrodden, everyday folk that struggled to put bread on the table.

Never had a sense of 'them and us' felt so apparent. The gap between the *have's and the have fuck-all's* opened-up like a festering wound. The country was on the brink of civil war.

In Yorkshire, and other coal mining communities, the workers were battered with more than just truncheon and boot as the pits that had provided the livelihood for young and old alike faced premature and forced closure. Towns and villages, once rich and vibrant, drew their last breath as the same blood that ran through the veins of its workers now coursed a bloody trail down the faces of those that dared to stand up and be counted.

Thousands fell as the war raged on. A battle played out under the gaze of a nation divided. Some felt that the miners were nothing more than marauding thugs, whilst others retched at the overzealous policing and the brutality that hid behind the cloak of the Law. Whatever, this was a war without a victor. And even though the mines were destined to close, those that dared to fight, came away with their dignity intact. Workers have nothing without pride, and in the end no baton or boot could crush those indomitable spirits.

It wasn't long after the UK became *Maggie's farm* that both my Dad and Mum were made redundant. The battles fought on the picket lines were over and the unions defeated. It felt like the whole of Liverpool was affected. There were no jobs to be had, and an area once proud became a graveyard filled with the hopes and dreams of a shattered and exhausted people.

Money was tight, but my Dad refused to sign-on and claim dole. Instead, he would offer to do odd jobs for people to make a few quid. He would do anything and everything in his power to put food on the table. We lived off the meagre savings that we had, until one day he declared that we were moving to Cumbria, where he had secured a job on a caravan site. Worse still, we were moving into a caravan and selling our house.

My first thought, as selfish as it now seems, was about my Karate training. I didn't want to move to Cumbria and be forced to find another place to train. I gave little thought to moving into a tin can that had no electricity or running water and, much worse, was in the middle of nowhere. Mum and my brother stayed at our house to oversee the sale, and I was packed off to deepest, darkest Cumbria with my Dad. No surprise there. I think Mum saw it as a reprise from the shit I was still giving her.

Nothing could prepare me for the culture shock of moving out of our comfortable 3-bed semi and into a cold, and cramped caravan.

I went from having friends I could walk out of our front door and see, to stepping out of a caravan door to be faced by fields full of sheep and cows. Caravans are a strange phenomenon, freezing in the winter and unbearably hot on the few and far between good summer days. In the winter, the park was closed, and we lived alone in our caravan, surrounded by the empty holiday homes of the normal people. Normal because they had proper homes to go back to after their weekend escape to the country, in their second home.

For my family, the camp site in the winter was a deathly silent graveyard. It felt more like a concentration camp than a holiday destination, and even the summer months were hardly buzzing. It was, after all, a few fields with caravans on. The nearest shop was a 3-mile hike and the nearest town 7 miles away. Bath times were interesting, to say the least. I had to walk down a grass slope to the laundry room and have a bath in a tin container originally used for feeding cattle that was filled (slowly) by kettle.

If it was raining, I was far dirtier by the time I got back up the hill than before I went for the bath. This was to be my reality for over 3 years. We lived on the breadline, trying to make the best of a terrible situation. I forgot what it was like to be able to flick a switch and have instant light, or to watch a TV that wasn't powered by a car battery (it always went flat, just at the best bit of a film or show).

If the gas bottle ran out at 9.00pm on a Saturday night, it meant an early night, wrapped up in blankets to try and keep warm. Sleep on a particularly windy or wet night was almost an impossible task as the noise on the tin roof was unbearable. And then there was the ever-present threat of break ins.

In the closed season we had to patrol the site at night to make sure the vans were secure. Armed with just a torch, my Dad would head one way and I would go the other. We had been the victim of a break-in ourselves. One Christmas eve, the owner of the site had invited us to his plush farmhouse for Christmas dinner. We had a few meagre presents under the small tree in our caravan that we had managed to get each other (probably through the catalogue) and a few decorations that we had kept from the normal world.

It was heartbreaking for my Mother to see the place ransacked on our return, with all our stuff (such as it was) either gone or broken, and worse, the intruders took it upon themselves to trash the place. Mud was smeared over the walls and settee. Ornaments were broken and left scattered in a thousand pieces. Clothes were ripped-up and tossed aside, photographs smashed and trodden underfoot.

I never understood (and still don't) how someone could go out and rob from a family that were obviously poorer than themselves. At least, that's how I imagined it. They probably lived in a house with electricity and a real bath. We were living on next to nothing, described, at the time, as being well-below the poverty line. There was working class and then, if relegated a division down like we were, you became a member of the underclass. We were so poor, we had no chance of replacing the items smashed, ripped and defiled. The Police had an idea of who had done the burglary, but nothing came of it (maybe if we were not viewed as gypsies and beneath society it would be different).

I remembered the name they bandied about, and a few years later, I was to take the law into my own hands and make the thief pay for the pain he had caused my family.

6

Daydream Believer

"Yes, I am a dreamer. For a dreamer is one who can only find his way in moonlight, and his punishment is that he sees the dawn before the rest of the world." Oscar Wilde

It was obvious, even to a 13-year-old, that my Dad was being royally shafted by the owner of the campsite. A fat, ruddy-faced fellow with the strangest accent I had ever heard, he seemed to sing words and punctuate the end of every sentence with a deep intake of breath.

He and his Mrs lived in a big farmhouse, drove top of the range cars and generally wanted for nothing. Dad worked from 7.00am until the sun went down and, even then, was rarely in until gone 9.00pm. Not for him a 5-day week, he worked every day. The pay should have reflected the number of hours he did and the level of commitment but, unfortunately, it didn't. Not by a long shot. There was minimum wage and then there was the meagre pay my old man got. He was not in the first flush of youth either, he had been well into his forties when I was born.

Luckily, he was incredibly fit. His main job in the summer months meant pushing a large petrol mower up and down the many hills on the camp site. That, and doing everything else the red-faced, tight bastard told him to do. Any savings we had following the sale of our house soon went and we were always living hand to mouth. I did some labouring on a farm in the summer to earn some cash, but it really wasn't enough to put us back up to good old Division 3 working class. The only good thing for me was the time I spent away from school. The 6 months I lived initially with my Dad, I never went to school. Instead, I learned to drive the battered old truck we used for collecting the garbage and helped Dad with his bin round.

In the Summer, I practiced my Kata in the fields like some renegade monk, 'Kwai Chang Savage'. I became depressed because I wasn't training properly and all attempts to find a Shotokan club proved fruitless. There was a Wado Ryu Karate club 7 miles up the road in Cockermouth. I joined it more out of desperation than a need to change styles. I was told my stance was too long and I needed to concentrate more on speed of movement. I enjoyed it, but it wasn't my beloved Shotokan.

Changing secondary schools was interesting, to say the least, when eventually my Mum arrived and made me go. My accent was mimicked by the local kids, who called me *Gypo* and other derogatory terms for a caravan dweller (I was part Romany Gypsy on my Mum's side, so always took offence to these remarks). The confrontations invariably ended with me throwing a punch and walking out of school.

My Mum was at the end of her tether with me again, fighting daily and, worse, walking out. Eventually, people started to get the message that I wasn't anyone's punch bag and, if pushed, would unleash my fists and feet of fury in true Bruce Lee style. I stopped eating, believing the jibes from my new tormentors that I was fat. My Mum sent me to school with sandwiches because we couldn't afford school dinners and every lunchtime, I would throw the sandwich in the bin. At night I would often make myself sick.

I woke early every day and did sit-ups until my stomach hurt. I was losing weight and was often close to passing out, but I took just enough food to get me through the day. I realised then how it felt to be on the other side. The bully became the bullied, a kind of full-circle social justice.

I didn't like this life and would dream of the day I could escape it. The only thing that kept me going was the drive to be like Bruce Lee. I wanted to become as famous as he was. I longed to be an actor and martial arts star. I even sent a letter to the Royal Academy of Dramatic Art asking if I could enrol. Mum had told me that anyone that was anyone in the film business had gone there.

Eventually, a letter arrived at the caravan park, postmarked from the Royal Academy. I couldn't bring myself to open it and asked my Mum to tell me what it said. I knew things were not going to plan when she started laughing and, after handing it to Dad, I saw him shake his head in disbelief. The letter was very polite but, as I was only 14 years old, apparently, I would need to wait another 4 years before auditioning. The fee per term was in the thousands, so given that we struggled to put food on the table, it was well out of reach. My Dad said that I should stop daydreaming and get my head out of the clouds.

It might sound harsh, but my parents had been brought up in a different time. If they had only realised that daydreaming was the only thing that was keeping me alive. Without dreams, what is the point? Reality was hard. I was determined it wouldn't drag me down though. As Oscar Wilde said, "We are all in the gutter, only some of us are looking up at the stars."

Despite my parent's advice, my gaze was firmly fixed and locked skywards.

7

Dedicated Follower of Fashion

"Our wisdom comes from our experience, and our experience comes from our foolishness." Sacha Guitry

It was just before we moved to Cumbria that I finally got to see a Bruce Lee film.

Fist of Fury. I remember it with a sense of both glee and embarrassment. My brother convinced me that, if I wore his platform shoes, flared trousers, and he drew on a pencil moustache with Mum's eyebrow pencil, I would breeze past the ticket booth, looking 18. No worries.

I know it sounds ludicrous, but I went along with it (my brother was very convincing). So, there I was, teetering on four-inch heels, pencil moustache (literally) adorning my top lip, waiting for a bus to take me to the flea pit cinema in Maghull.

Amazingly, it worked. Or, so I thought. In my best impression of a grown man's voice I said, "One please."

I thought I saw a couple of nods, winks and giggles from people in the queue, and the lad in the booth gave me a big smile before handing me my ticket, but I didn't care, I was in. That first scene, Bruce Lee in his white suit running through the rain before diving atop the grave of his teacher will stay with me for the rest of my days.

As will the sound of laughter from my Mum and Brother when I made it home (miraculously, given that those shoes were a death trap, and I looked like a parody of 40's film star Ronald Coleman) to triumphantly tell how I had only gone and pulled it off and no one had suspected a thing. It was at this point that my Mum told me that she had gone into the cinema the day before and bribed the lad on the ticket booth to let me in, that I saw it all clearly, a chance to have a little bit of fun at Junior's expense.

I still didn't care. All that mattered was that I had seen my first Bruce Lee film, and it didn't disappoint. Also, I thought, I looked okay with a 'tache. The disguise may have been worthy of a villain in a Scooby Doo episode, but at least I didn't have to say, "I'd have gotten away with it too, were it not for you pesky kids."

8

Walls Come Tumbling Down

"The worse the Passage, the more welcome the Port." Thomas Fuller

My family's time of living in abject poverty was nearly at an end, or so we thought.

The fat campsite owner convinced my Dad to build a bungalow which he said we could move into as a reward for Dad's hard work. And better, he promised that we would have electricity and running water.

I was 16 years old, ready to leave school and I still didn't have a clue what to do with my life. Well, that's not entirely true. I had still harboured dreams to become an actor. The country was still royally fucked-up and jobs for a 16-year-old school leaver, armed with an 'O' level in English and a head full of dreams, were few and far between.

I eventually got a job in a Hotel. I was the Kitchen Porter, which in layman's terms meant that I was a general dogsbody, or chief washer-upper. The owner of the Hotel was an absolute knob. He was basically a bully that thought he was God's gift to mankind. I lived in a cramped bedsit above a noisy pub, though to be honest, after living in a caravan for three years, it felt like a palace.

The owner of the Hotel made me work around the clock. I would stagger up to my room, exhausted, and try to sleep above the raucous carry-on that came from the pub downstairs. I lasted about a month before losing my temper with God's gift. He had asked me to clean up his dog's mess. It wasn't just the request that sent me into meltdown. I had already worked 12 hours and been on the receiving end of his vile tongue for most of the shift.

Long story short, he nearly ended up wearing a large saucepan and was told to clean up his own shit. I walked out and trekked the 7 miles home in the pitch black, but I felt liberated. I made a vow, then and there, that no-one would make me feel so worthless again. Suffice to say, my parents were less than happy to get a knock on their door in the early hours only to be told I had walked out of my first real job.

Anyhow, I wasn't to live at home for long, as fate, often, has a way of pulling the rug from beneath your feet.

I came home one day to find my Mum crying at the kitchen table. We had only been in this bungalow for a couple of years, but it seemed that after getting my Dad to build the house, old ruddy cheeks decided to give my Dad's job and the house to his local pub landlord after he had been laid off by the brewery. While Mum cried, Dad went into a spin. I had never seen him so angry.

We were given a week to vacate the property, but we had nowhere to go and no money to rent anywhere. The old man decided to barricade us in – the Dunkirk Spirit had kicked-in and he wasn't going down without a fight.

The fat owner stayed away, stupidly sending my Dad's replacement to try and get us out. Not a good move given that my Dad was ready to kill someone. Whilst Dad and I manned the fort, my Mother was desperately trying to find accommodation.

The Council didn't want to know, advising that, once we left the house, we would be put on a list and possibly get put into a temporary homeless shelter. Her tenacity paid off when one of the jobs she had been applying for said they could come for an interview. The job was in the West Midlands, working as caretakers in a United Reformed Church, and a flat was thrown in with the deal, so it looked good for them. The only downside was that it was a flat and job for a couple, so I couldn't go with them.

I advised them to go for it. I could look after myself and, if needed, could move into a small flat (look after myself - that was a laugh, I couldn't cook, wash clothes or iron). And that's exactly what happened. Well, after my Dad had given his replacement a right-hander.

The family was split, with me in Cockermouth, my brother in Halesowen and my parents moving to Birmingham. Life can make you grow up fast sometimes, and this was certainly one of those times. I watched their small car, packed to the roof with all their worldly goods, drive away, and wondered what I was going to do now. My Dad had given me a couple of hundred quid from the settlement they had forced out of old red cheeks and made me promise to call him if I needed anything. The saying, *'what doesn't kill you makes you stronger'* is certainly true, but what they don't tell you is that, whilst you are waiting for this inner strength, you are literally shitting yourself.

The support network had headed down the M6, leaving me to fend for myself. After finding a job in a local factory, I started to find my feet and enjoyed the freedom that I had. I even learned to iron quite well and was a whizz in the kitchen, so long as the menu was simple and came with instructions on the back of the box.

9

Smells Like Teen Spirit

"There aren't a lot of opportunities for that rite of passage that makes you a man. War is one of them, and violent sports are another." Sylvester Stallone

1980. John Lennon is gunned down outside the Dakota Building in New York City. The American people elect former B-movie star Ronald Reagan as their President and, in the UK, the average house price rises to a colossal £13,650.

I stayed with the Wado Ryu Karate for a couple of years, but it never felt right to me. I had also started to question the arts' practicality, particularly after I got into a fight after class one night.

Some local wannabe bikers were watching the lesson and laughing and generally taking the piss out of us. I decided to have a polite word, something along the lines of, 'go forth and multiply'. This went down like a sausage at a Vegetarian Society lunch and the great unwashed were far from impressed with my rather candid approach.

Colin (yes, you read it right) the leader, told me he was going to kick my head in, to which I laughed and went back to class. After the lesson I was walking a young lady that I had recently become romantically involved with home, when, out of the shadows, stepped Colin and his band of merry (if somewhat smelly) men.

Colin wanted to fight, and I wasn't going to disappoint. After all, I was a Purple Belt in Karate, so what could go wrong?

Colin may have had all the grace of an elephant on smack, but he executed a near perfect rugby tackle that had me on my back and deflecting his clubbing hands from my face. I managed, somehow, to turn him onto his back and got in a few punches of my own, but that was when things turned ugly. Colin's cronies decided that they didn't like to see their glorious leader getting a thumping, and one of them - let's call him greasy-haired fat bloke, or *GHFB* for short, decided that he would try out his new Doc Marten boots on my head. The first kick put me in a spin and allowed Colin the chance to get up. Surprisingly, this is where the story gets a little strange.

Instead of using his new-found position to pummel the living daylights out of me, Colin stopped the fight and admonished GHFB for his cowardly action.

I was a bit bloodied, as was Colin, but at that moment I admired his sense of fair play. We shook hands and later became friends (sort of). There was a mutual respect anyway, and we often joked about our one-on-one battle every time we saw each other. We could never be close mates; I hated the music and culture of the rockers. I also hated the fact that I had been on the receiving end of a poorly-planned attack.

I thought I could take on the world - I had karate, after all - but, the fight with Colin really opened my eyes. My Dad had always maintained that a self-defence system had to be effective in any situation. I remembered the example of an attack in a phone box.

"How are you going to be able to kick someone in a confined space? What if it goes off and you are in a phone box?"

I didn't have the answer way back then, and I certainly didn't have it now. I started to look at other scenarios, such as my recent encounter with Colin and his Neanderthal hit squad. I knew that I could take and give a punch, but what about close-quarter and ground fighting? I was lucky to have reversed Colin - God knows how I had done it - but I was lucky. And, what if Colin had not turned out to possess any moral fibre and let his goons kick me unconscious?

Or worse still, they had killed me.

10

Heartbreak Hotel

"If music be the food of love, play on. Give me excess of it, that surfeiting. The appetite may sicken, and so die."
William Shakespeare

I didn't ponder on the fight with Colin and his band of brothers for long as I was about to get my first dose of teenage heartbreak.

Karen was my first love and, at the point that she ended our summer love story, I thought that I was destined to forever wander this earth alone. I genuinely believed that she was *the one*. She had met my parents and I hers. We even had a special place that we would meet, a song that was *our tune* and sometimes we even finished each other's sentences (pass the sick bag)

But we came from different worlds. Hers was organised, assured, middle class, whereas I was from the wrong side of the tracks, an all too brief distraction before she headed off to University and a career. I had little idea as to where my future lay. University might as well have been the moon. I hadn't dared to tell Karen that I really wanted to be an actor, the laughter from my Mum when she read my RADA letter still echoed around my head.

My apparent lack of ambition didn't exactly endear me to her parents either. I could tell that they were less than happy with their daughter's choice in boyfriend. I further alienated myself one night, shortly after our great romance had hit the rocks, when I turned up on their doorstep, drunk, and demanding to see their daughter. My only saving grace was that the kick I aimed at their locked door didn't do any damage, other than to my already deflated ego.

Young love's course is said to run less than smoothly. My heart was broken, and I couldn't see a way to fix it other than to drown my sorrows with copious amounts of alcohol. It was a vicious circle really. I would get drunk and try to convince Karen to take me back. She in, turn, would run further from me. When you are young and heartbroken it seems like the whole world has ended. You can't see past your tears and refuse to listen to those wise words from others that have walked the same dark road. The pain of a teenage broken heart feels worse than any broken bone. But, that sense of loss is something that most of us feel at some point in our lives. It is a necessary part of growing up, a rite of passage.

I have seen many a so-called *hard man* brought to his knees as the result of unrequited love. Grown men suddenly struck down, incapable of reason or rhyme. The tough guy image drops faster than a falling star when they check into heartbreak hotel and there occurs a metamorphic change. The teenage rampage slows to a meander and the thrashing guitars of exuberant youth and rebellion are replaced by the heavenly sounds of a thousand harps. Self-pity is worn like a medal, a reminder of a battle that was fought and lost.

That pain can be multiplied a thousand-fold the first time you bump into your saintly Ex and her new love. It happened to me about a month into my 'mooning about' phase. This is the part of the break-up where you can't eat or sleep and the only music you listen to is 'your song' (repeatedly).

Your soul has been ripped out and you have been possessed by the ghost of Aled Jones in his choirboy years. Any fight you had, any fire, is extinguished as you see yourself as 'the victim'. Hard done to, misunderstood. You become a shadow of your former self.

Anyway, I digress. The first time I saw Karen and her latest love-sick pup was in a local nightclub. I was in full teenage angst mode, my now self-pitying persona glowing, emitting a kind of invisible forcefield that keeps people at arm's length, when across the dance floor I saw her. My shattered heart lurched, and, for a brief moment, I thought, "This is fate." Our reunion, the fairy-tale ending where we got back together, and I carried Karen off on a white steed (not that I could ride a horse, even if I had one). Only that wasn't to happen. At her side I saw a face I recognised as 'Bob' or, as he was locally known, 'Bumbo'.

How the hell could this happen? I had been replaced by a bloke that was happy to be called 'Bumbo'. They were caught up in the moment, dancing to Ottawan's, "Hand's Up", a stupid song that made me want to commit murder every time it was played.

Bumbo was breaking out his best moves, his mouth was full of glowing white teeth and his haircut was common for the day - long over one eye (think early Spandau Ballet). His carrot pants made him look like a demented Cossack and, for the life of me, I couldn't see the attraction.

They pumped their hands in the air as one, their smiles almost dazzled brighter than the disco ball that spun above their heads. And then it happened, Bumbo pulled her close, his colossal mouth closed in like a Great White shark going in for the kill and they locked lips. I half expected the theme tune from Jaws to strike up.

I knew then that it was over. My self-pity turned to rage and, as Bumbo twirled and gyrated to the sound of Ottawan, I turned on my heel and walked away. Not so much as a backward glance. There's no better medicine than a good old case of reality, washed down with a chaser of anger and betrayal. I could have given Bumbo a right-hander but imagine the cost of the dental bill had those pearly whites been separated from his mush.

Had I knocked out those gnashers he could always have changed his name to Gumbo, I supposed.

11

This is the Modern World

"The invention of the teenager was a mistake. Once you identify a period of life in which people get to stay out late but don't have to pay taxes- naturally, no one wants to live any other way." Judith Martin

It was around this time in my life that I put Martial Arts on the backburner and started to go further off the rails.

I got caught up in the Mod movement that was enjoying a revival, riding a Vespa scooter, drinking and dancing at all-nighters to the Northern Soul music that, along with The Jam, provided the soundtrack to my misspent youth.

Along with the subculture of Modernism went the battles between teenage and young adolescents that have been a part of our history and heritage for hundreds of years. We got into fights with National Front Skinheads, Bikers and, at other times, we fought each other. We were the epitome of angry young men, riding our scooters up and down the country in search of another weekend thrill, which usually culminated in a fight or being kicked out of whichever town we had rolled into atop our two-stroke chariots.

I had learned my lessons well, especially one of the best bits of advice on self-defence my Dad ever imparted, "Hit first, hit hard and keep hitting until the fight is over."

I got it off to a fine art. Usually the fracas would start in the usual way.

"Oi Mod, are all you lot gay then?"

Or, "Why do you lot ride them fanny wagons/hairdryers?"

I never really let them get any further than the first couple of words before throwing a few punches into the mix. At this point things often escalated into a mass brawl between the two warring factions and invariably ended up with Police and ambulance crews being called.

I had a real *wake up and smell the coffee* moment when, one night, I bumped into someone in a bar (literally). Although I apologised, this bloke, who I later found out to be from the travelling community, was having none of it.

"Outside," he spat in a broad Irish accent.

I looked around. I couldn't chin him there and then, there were bouncers and, worse, too many potential witnesses. And I didn't want to get banned from the pub or locked up.

I looked for my mates, thinking, "If this kicks-off and his mates jump in, I need backup."

They were around but otherwise engaged in chatting up the local talent, or just getting pissed out of their skulls. Either way, I was on my own.

"One on one?", I said.

"Meet me in five minutes on the car park," the Traveller nodded. A strange request, but at least it gave me time to finish my JD and Coke.

The time of the *straightener* came around. I strode through the crowd, excited to fight, but with the usual knot in my stomach. Not fear, as such, more a feeling of *what if*? The fear of the unknown. I had had this feeling many times, but this time something didn't feel right.

The doors swung open and there he was in the centre of the small car park. My opponent - cocky and confident, large as life and twice as ugly. I knew that these travellers liked to box, and his orthodox stance gave away his intention to give me a right-hander at the earliest opportunity.

I didn't wait. Rushing across the car park, I fired off a right cross that staggered him but didn't put him down. The next thing I felt, after the connection of my knuckles and his head, was a sudden and violent blow to the side of my face. Time went to that slow motion feeling you get when caught by an unexpected punch.

It took me a while to realise that the punch had not come from my Irish friend, but from his mate who had been hiding in the shadows. I turned to confront the coward but, as I did, my original opponent dragged me to the ground. Throughout the ensuing brutal beating I remember looking towards the pub doors. There, gathered with noses pressed to the glass as if watching a stranger getting his face rearranged, were my so-called mates, frozen by their fear, but unable to look away.

The two Irish lads were now taking it in turn to jump on my head, obviously enjoying an evening of practicing their best Irish dance moves like two demented Michael Flatley chorus liners. Heavy feet stamped the imprint of their dodgy shoes onto my face. I was a mess, choking as the blood from my shattered nose ran down my throat, causing me to gargle and gasp for breath.

Eventually, after what seemed like hours but was probably less than a couple of minutes, the beating stopped. A siren sounded in the distance, signalling the arrival of either the Police or the ambulance service and thankfully interrupting the Irish lad's fun, setting them running like hares chased by a pack of hounds.

I got to my feet and assessed the damage which probably looked worse than it felt and made off in the opposite direction. I was hurt, but at least I was okay. There would be no arrest or hospital bed for me that night, but I knew that this fight would be an experience I would never forget. Some lessons are hard to take, and some are just downright brutal. This lesson was in both categories.

As for my so-called mates, I understood them not getting involved. I had gone out with a bunch of lads that were not my usual brothers-in-arms. They were not the foot soldiers that revelled in the many weekend battles, rather they were the hangers-on, happy to talk a good fight but nowhere to be seen when the proverbial shit hit the fan. I knew that had my best mate, Frank, been there, then the situation would have ended differently. There are times when you must stand alone (or in this case fall alone) and this was just one of those times.

Walking back through the town that night, my appearance solicited a few funny looks. I was aware that my nose was broken and one eye closed, but I was more annoyed at the fact that my new 3-button, Italian-cut, dog-tooth check suit was ruined. I could take looking like I had been involved in a head-on crash with a bus, but the ruined suit really pissed me off.

Being a Mod and a fighter was never a marriage made in Heaven.

The Punks and Rockers didn't care what they looked like, but to a Mod, clothes were a statement. They defined our religion and we worshipped at the altar of Mod.

It was a strange paradox that, together with the music, the scooter and the sharp clothes, went the often-mindless violence. The Mods confused a lot of the other factions that were about in the 80's. We probably looked a bit effeminate, with our immaculate clothes, penchant for wearing eyeliner and riding a mode of transport that bucked against the trend for loud, fast and greasy motorcycles or souped-up cars. The truth was that most (but not all) of the lads I knew that rode scooters and took a pride in their appearance could have a ruck. Looking like we did, it was necessary to be a bit handy, or at least be around lads that were.

But, at the end of the day, we were all the same, regardless of which cult we identified with. We were just confused young men and women, all looking for something to belong to, something to define us, make us different from our parents and past generations (we weren't any different really, just born in a different time). Call it a way of life, or just a natural part of being young, rebellious, and growing up in a capitalist country, the expectation is to follow the norms and values that society sets.

As Mods, we shunned the mass movement that is respectability. Throughout the ages, the wheels have kept turning and the working classes are kept in their place. Rewarded at the weekend by a small pay packet that invariably finds its way into the tills of the pubs and clubs that can offer an escape from the drudgery of the working week.

James Dean, the original *Rebel Without a Cause*, had a lot to answer for. Thanks to Dean, it had become trendy to be misunderstood, moody and kicking against the hypothetical walls that were built to keep us from breaking away. In fact, it was expected.

Fighting was an English tradition. When there were no wars to go to, we fought each other, either as a result of which group and faction we belonged to, or which football team we followed. The crime? Being different. Different musical taste, clothes, haircuts. It didn't register that we were too busy fighting our own kind, whilst the privileged few scowled behind the safety of the net curtains and chintz-absorbed lives. Those so-called ruling classes that wore respectability like a second skin.

The real irony, of course, was that the rich kids wanted to be like us. They envied the way we looked and lived. They wanted to rebel, but Mummy and Daddy would probably stop their allowance and disinherit them if they went too far. Some, the 'artier' ones, tried but it was just a phase. A bit like a gap year, acting like an oik before conformity set in and they were packed off to University.

I disliked this type more than the rich kids that looked at us from a perceived vantage point. The 'wannabes' or 'plastics' never had a clue what it meant to be a Mod, a Skin or a Rock-a-Billy. The youth cults were the property of the working classes. The one thing we owned and understood above all else. Money can buy a lot of things, but it can't buy membership to the working class. Yes, working man fought working man, but we respected each other. Fighting was for the weekend and it was a given that we would lock horns with our rivals. It was expected that we would defend our beliefs, stand our ground, no matter the cost (usually our liberty).

Whatever the outcome, we never 'grassed'. We had our own ways of 'evening-up' the scores; a code of ethics that we lived by. We were judge, jury and executioner all rolled into one. And I, for one, would rather take a beating and bide my time than talk to the Police. I was, and still am, a believer in Karma - *what goes around comes around*. And my time with the 'Flatley' brothers would come (well, with one of them, anyway).

I got locked up a few times during this period of my life. Despite my growing criminal record, I didn't think about the consequences of future employment. With youth comes ignorance, a kind of invincibility cloak that shields you from the reality of your actions, at least for a time. Having said that, there is nothing worse than the morning after you have been involved in a fight or some other misdemeanour. Your mind is in turmoil, thinking about the previous night's escapade. Did I hurt the person badly? What if they are in hospital or, worse, dead?

And then there was the waiting. The waiting for the familiar knock on the door. A sound that could only be a Police Knock.

It sounds odd, but I knew instinctively when the Police were at the door and, on opening, I guessed they weren't there for a donation to the Police benevolent fund. The day after lock-up was far worse than the night of the crime lock-up. The adrenaline had worn off, like a cheap cologne, to be replaced by a strange mix of shame, self-loathing and loneliness. You were on your own. No mates to egg you on. The pride you felt the night before, fighting the good fight, was over. The sugar pedestal had melted. The audience had long gone, leaving you centre stage, the spotlight shining on your crime, now the property of the critics.

Of course, when you got bailed, you bulled it up. Sitting in the pub holding court with your mates. Tales of how you had laughed at the Police, giving them nothing but abuse and yadda, yadda, yadda... There's Dutch Courage, whereby you use alcohol to get the minerals to do something, and then there is the other kind of courage that is fuelled by the need to be accepted, even admired, for your actions. A need to continually prove yourself as fearless. Hard.

Unfortunately, I suffered the latter. Always the first to run into the crowd and the last to be dragged out. And, when the deed was done, the fight or other laddish act was dissected over a beer, creating a legend to be toasted by your peers. The tale invariably got distorted as it was passed from person to person. A kind of Chinese whisper syndrome. Being arrested, once the feeling of 'Oh shit' had passed, became a badge of honour. Making the front page of the local paper only added to the hype that surrounded you and served as a permanent record for the scrap book.

The Mod scene was thriving in West Cumbria, and its most ardent followers stayed the course through the many fashion changes and dodgy haircuts that permeated the 80's in the UK. I had started a serious relationship with a girl I had met in a nightclub one Saturday night. She wasn't a Modette, but there was something about her that caught my attention. We soon went from flirtation to a serious item.

Joan was great company and, it must be said, she wasn't bad to have around if a fight broke out. One night we were in a club called Trader Bill's, a seedy dive that was full of head cases. Mostly idiots that I, at some point, had given a right-hander to. One group the Mods had beef with were a charming bunch of Neanderthals called 'The Annie Pit Lads', a gang of hardened brawlers that hated anyone that wasn't from 'the pit'. It didn't matter what faction you were, these morons hated on everybody that wasn't in their clique.

The Mods had had some legendary battles with these charming men. My best mate, Frank, had recently parted one of the main lads' hair with a table, which obviously hadn't endeared us to them. The upshot was they were looking for revenge and, if Frank wasn't about, then any of us Mods would do. It was an odd night in the club, usually there would be a few of the lads in, but not this night. I stuck out like a sore thumb in my Prince of Wales check suit, white button-down shirt, wool tie held in place by a vintage tie clip and black and white Shelly shoes (very dapper).

Most revellers that night sported those long, over one eye haircuts, carrot pants and ruffle shirts favoured by the New Romantics (Bumbo style), which, had there actually had been a fashion Police, these *Herbert's* would all be doing serious time. If I stood out, then so too did the twenty-strong group of 'Pittians'.

Someone needed a word about their distinct lack of style, not to mention their pungent aroma. These lads hadn't gone out to 'enjoy' the soothing tones of Spandau Ballet or Boy George (not that I had, either), their purpose was to chat-up the local girls, swill copious amounts of ale and have a good scrap before the perfunctory kebab and going home to their bedsits. I was immediately on their radar, and I could see them scanning the room to see if I had any back up.

"It's about to go off," I exclaimed.

Joan knew it too and you could cut the atmosphere with a knife. The great unwashed were blocking the only exit, staring at me and occasionally pointing and laughing. I knew I was in for a beating and therefore had nothing to lose. Telling Joan to stay back (not that she listened), I walked straight over to my welcoming party.

There was a sense of excitement coupled with a little apprehension bubbling inside. To this day I'm not sure why I did what came next, but life is full of questions that don't always have, or need, an answer. I stood on one leg (think the 'Karate Kid' pose), smiling and gesturing the group forwards with upturned palm. The look on their faces was priceless, but I didn't get long to savour the moment as they rushed forward, fists flying at me from all angles. I, in turn, hit out at anything that moved, connecting with one or two good shots before I was dragged to the floor and unceremoniously beaten to a pulp.

Even on the ground I aimed kicks at anything that looked like a ball bag which, to be honest, was all the gang. It is usually like this in a fight, time seems to go into slow-motion, with the punches and kicks bouncing off your face, head and body. From within this surreal existence it is possible to make out sounds. Mostly screams from your *other half*. There is no other way to describe this scenario other than it must feel a lot like drowning (remember, I had almost drowned as kid), being swept away by a powerful current before the blackness of the water envelopes your whole being.

Eventually, the punches and kicks subside, and you regain wobbly legs. My first thought usually is my suit, but on this occasion, I knew that Joan, more than likely, had swung off one of these nut-jobs necks, clawing, biting and screaming as she did so. Joan was fine. I was a bit bloody and bruised but other than that, no permanent damage. The Pit lads had legged-it before the Police turned up, and another night had ended in a ruck, my bruises a badge of honour for going at the gang single-handedly and living to tell the tale. But damn, another Carnaby Street suit ruined.

I didn't have long to wait to even up the score. The following Sunday I was drinking in a less than salubrious watering hole that carried the kind of reputation that acted like a cross to a vampire to the respectable punter. If there wasn't a fight at the end of the night, it was the gossip of the town the next day. I was in good company. A few of the lads and a handful of the proper Skinheads, not the racist stereotypes that had adopted the look and worshipped Hitler, (remember him, the little fella with a poor excuse for a moustache, the despot my Dad had garroted in a phone box?). Anyway, I digress. The jukebox was on full volume and the pub was bouncing, with everyone in great form.

I looked across the room and caught sight of one of the faces that ran the Pit crew. He was a well-known bully. A real piece of work. I pushed my way through the crowd and stood in front of him, my face inches from his (which, given the fact that he had halitosis, wasn't pleasant).

"What's your problem?" he spat, trying to disguise the quiver in his voice.

"Remember me?" I countered.

It wasn't so much a question as a statement. He looked even stupider as he struggled to take in the words. I launched at him, our bodies connecting with the sort of force that a good prop forward would have been proud of. The impact sent us over the table and beyond as half-empty beer glasses and ashtrays smashed onto the already beer-sticky floor. I wasted no time in raining down some good hard shots as I straddled the now cowering 'tough guy'. Blood sprayed from his nose as its' bone structure crumbled beneath my now-bruised knuckles.

He was gurgling as the claret washed down his throat. My elbow arched skyward ready to finish my mini makeover of his already ugly mush, but I felt hands pulling me backwards and soon I was back on my feet being held by three or four of my mates. I wasn't quite finished. I saw my target try to regain his footing. He was hunched on all fours, grabbing wildly for something steady enough to pull him to his feet.

He almost made it too, but for the solid connection of my right foot with his jaw.

He was done. His prone body lay shrouded by broken glass and fag ends, a drinker's version of a snow angel. Brutality is the best weapon against this type of low life. Yes, there would likely be recriminations, but this was the way it was. It went with the territory. He who lives by the sword and all that.

People often talk about posturing before a fight, that moment before the first push or punch. In all the fights I had been in, I knew well the feeling you get before it goes off. Your stomach turns and lurches, a tremor or shake in the hands and legs and perhaps a bead of sweat on the forehead. Posturing is the fighter's way of hiding these traits. The best or most experienced fighters had it off to a fine art and knew that it was a fight-winning strategy to unnerve their opponent. You see it all the time in professional bouts. Think Conor McGregor or, back in the day, Muhammad Ali, both masters of the trash-talking and posturing game. In the street people are often beaten before a punch is thrown by perceived images. Look at the trend for bouncers to be heavily-muscled or for the Skinheads penchant for shaved heads and tattoos. Both are a way of trying to make the statement 'don't fuck with me', but both can often reveal, to the trained eye, that beneath the camouflage there is a scared person desperate to frighten away potential threats before they start.

It's the reason I was always quick to hit first and fast. I didn't want to get into the mental warfare that drags out the inevitable battle. So, when you did fight or deal with the type of scum where reprisals were common, you had to make a statement. After I was beaten up by the Pit lads, I had no choice. These lads were just like anyone, they felt safe in their packs, but get them alone and it would be a different story. There would be no statement made had the lad I had just pummelled come out of the skirmish with a fat lip and dented pride. He had to be unrecognisable, a swollen and battered reminder that said, 'beat me and I would be back'.

And it didn't matter how many times it happened, the rest of his crew should be fearful that the same fate awaited them. It's the law of the jungle that I was living in. Fair play was for others. As Bruce Lee said, "Adapt or be destroyed." If you weren't prepared to be this way, you had better like hospital food or, at least, get used to some sleepless nights.

These were heady times. I was fighting most weekends, waking up covered in bruises to both my body and, at times, my ego. In many regards the fights we had were fair. If we had a problem, we would sort it out with a 'straightener'. Mostly, the rucks ended without need for hospitalisation but, on occasion, it was inevitable. We were caught up in a vicious circle. We, as a group of like-minded young men, felt the need to defend the faith of being a Mod. Those that couldn't handle the constant threat of attack left the scene. They only played at it anyway, a true Mod lived it. It wasn't something you wore at weekends like a badge, it was inside you. Even if you wanted to change you couldn't. You didn't choose Mod, it chose you.

The weekends belonged to the young. If you were lucky enough to work, you had a few quid to spare on those essentials that the Mods needed to survive. That being enough to buy new threads, money for a few beers and entry to a club, and petrol money to fuel the scooter. On arranged weekends and Bank Holidays we packed sleeping bags onto the backs of our scooters and headed up the B-roads to some poor, unsuspecting coastal destination. Thousands of Mods, Skinheads and Scooter Boys congregated in the town, riding proudly up and down the seafront, filling the air as we went with the fumes from our two-stroke engines.

We slept anywhere that we could, not that we slept much during the weekend. Toilet blocks, bus shelters and alleyways being some of my past hotels of choice. It's a good thing that Trip Advisor wasn't about back in the day. One time I woke up on a grass slope and was horrified to discover that a slug had crawled across my face, leaving me looking like an extra in an Adam and The Ants video.

The locals stayed away from us mostly, fearing that we might start trouble. But, in the main, these Scooter runs were peaceful affairs. We came to drink, dance at the all-nighters, meet like-minded people to admire their clothes and scooters and, in turn, peacock our own style.

Occasionally, we would get some issues with local Biker gangs. These individuals, that we labelled 'the great unwashed', were mostly a few years older than us. They would ride up to our scooters and make out that they were going to try and kick us off, or their pillion passenger would produce a long bike chain that was held out in a threatening manner (they had obviously watched 'The Wild Bunch' too many times). The Mods, in turn, would open their toolbox (a neat little place to hide a variety of weapons) and wave whatever we had back in their faces (usually a spanner or hammer, something you could explain to the Police if searched). It was all a bit of a ritual really. Rarely did it come to someone getting kicked off their scooter or a weapon being used. The Rockers were just like us, other than their distinct lack of style and aversion to soap. All they wanted was the escape that these ride-outs offered. A chance to escape the realities that we lived in. For us it was all about getting away. We couldn't afford holidays, but these weekend trips were a release, something to bridge the gap between the harsh reality of the working week and the freedom that Friday night brought.

The sight of thirty Mods or more, wending their way through towns and villages on Vespa's and Lambretta's, a *green army* of young men and women intent on making the most of their youth, was something to behold. The often-inclement British weather couldn't, and wouldn't, dampen our enthusiasm. We were young, and our heads hadn't yet been polluted with all the things that so-called 'respectable society' deemed as sensible or expected. There was a time for all that 'acting like an adult' and this wasn't it. Youth was a gift that the Mod culture revered above all else, and most of us never looked further than the next weekend. The Who, the 60's spokespersons of the original Mod movement, said it all in their classic song 'My Generation', as an 18-year-old Roger Daltrey spits scorn into the faces of the so-called deriders of British youth culture with the line, "I hope I die before I get old".

We might not have had much but, we had our youth, and that was something that couldn't be taxed or stolen.

A Trick Up My Sleeve

The American Army Parkas that became the uniform of a legion of 80's Mods and served as a shield from the often cold and driving rain, were also useful for secreting things in with their baggy sleeves and pockets. Oftentimes, if a fight was about to start, we would bring out of our parkas a variety of *levellers*.

This was brought home once to a bunch of idiots that had followed one of the lads out of a club, intent on giving him a kicking. This particular lad, Paul, was small, slim, and didn't look like he could fight sleep, let alone a group of Neanderthals. I would have loved to have seen their faces when, from his parka sleeves, a pair of Nunchaku sticks appeared. He was good with them too, twirling them around his body like a Mod-version of Bruce Lee. Suffice to say he didn't get to part anyone's hair with them as they took to their feet.

I considered myself quite handy with the Nunchucks, practicing my Bruce Lee moves whenever I got the chance. But the day I nearly *crowned* the Old Man didn't end so well for me. The sticks had been twirling around me most of the day, I was in a hyper state and couldn't sit still despite my dad's prostration that he was trying to watch his favourite show, 'Question Time'. I moved closer to his armchair and playfully spun the sticks just above his head.

"Grace, sort this one out will you, he's driving me mad."

"Come on, Old Man, let's dance," I countered, letting out my finest Bruce war cry.

But, as he rose to give me a clip round the lug hole, the 'chucks caught him flush on the head, causing him to fall back onto the chair clutching his head, just as my mum walked into the room with a cup of tea in hand.

"Jesus, you little sod!" he exclaimed, before jumping up and grabbing the sticks out of my hands. "Right, Bruce Lee, let's see what you've got." It was obvious from the old man's face that junior was about to learn a valuable life lesson.

"Go on get your bloody Karate pyjamas on, let's dance," he said in a calm and quite unsettling way. Mum was obviously enjoying the unfolding spectacle and seemed particularly amused that I had parted dad's hair with the Nunchucks. So, here I was, standing in front of the old master, my karate suit worn like a suit of armour, my purple belt tied proudly around my waist. My opponent, wearing his favourite cardigan and carpet slippers, ready for the Royal Rumble. I was about 16 years old, cocky, thinking I could take the old boy into waters he had never been in. After all I wasn't the 10 year old boy, tapping out to his crafty wrist lock, I was a man, I even shaved every other week.

I took up a stance, ready to prove, once and for all, that my beloved karate was superior to my Dad's 'unarmed combat'. I danced around the living room occasionally flicking out a round house kick that was never in any danger of landing on its target. My confidence was growing.

"Can't catch me, old man, my Karate is too powerful," I said in my best impression of a badly dubbed Kung Fu movie star. I snaked out a lightning fast back fist which clipped the Yorkshire Dragon's left ear, the same spot that had taken the full force of my Nunchucks' attack. Something seemed to change in that moment as my dad side-stepped my next attack, effortlessly sweeping my lead leg as he went. My view changed quite rapidly as I flew into the air in what can only be described as that well-known technique, the 'arse over tit', and I found myself looking up at the ceiling with a carpet slipper pressed into my throat.

"Damn, let's go again old man," I said, with an air of misplaced cockiness. I got to my feet and stood opposite my nemesis and again took up my stance. This time I dropped into horse stance, legs out-stretched as I threw out a rapid ten or so crisp punches into the space between us. And that's where the fight ended for me and the valuable life lesson began, as the Yorkshire Dragon flicked his carpet slippered foot up and into my balls. Game, set, and match. The Nunchucks went back in the attic which now also housed my left testicle and I once again had to bow down to the superiority of the old man's skills.

12

Knockin' On Heaven's Door

"They say you die twice. One time when you stop breathing and a second time, a bit later, when somebody says your name for the last time." Banksy

It was a balmy summer's day, complete with an all-blue sky and shimmering tarmac. The kind of day that made you glad to be alive. I had picked up my best mate, Frank, on my trustee Vespa PX150, a beautiful machine that looked resplendent with its unusual burgundy spray job.

We were heading to the local scooter dealers with one of Frank's Vespa side panels; I think it needed a few dents knocking out, or something. I wasn't speeding, staying within the 30 miles an hour limit, enjoying the warm air on my face and the freedom that comes on two wheels atop a two-stroke engine. A bread van pulled over in front of me and, thinking he was parking, I pulled out to overtake. And that's when things went bad.

As I drew alongside the van he pulled out, knocking us off kilter. I struggled to keep the scooter upright but suddenly found myself sailing over the handlebars. I felt a massive and sudden impact on my chest and stomach as I landed on a wall. The force was so great that the wall crumbled under my body leaving me laying prone amongst the debris, gasping for air.

I must have passed out for a few seconds as the next thing I am aware of is people rushing towards me. Frank was standing over me and I could tell by the look on his face that I was in a bad way. Bizarrely, someone was removing my desert boots and Frank says that whoever it was walked off with them, but I'm not convinced that this part of the story wasn't Frank embellishing and later adding a bit of humour to events. By the time an ambulance arrived my lips had turned blue and I was slipping in and out of consciousness.

At the hospital I was rushed into the A&E Department. I could tell that people were milling around frantically working to save my life. A tube was inserted up my penis and another was pushed into a hole they had cut into my side. The pain was unbearable, and I was thinking that death would be the easy way out. I was told I was going to need surgery and, although I heard the words, they held no meaning. I was hastily sedated before the trolley ride to the theatre.

I awoke some hours later, tubes attached to my broken body. I opened my eyes to the sight of my parents staring blankly at me, but I was unable to talk, the pain so immense. I drifted in and out of sleep for the next day or so, waking one time to see a Catholic Priest standing over me. I panicked briefly before realising I am Church of England and, as far as I knew, we didn't get the Last Rites. The well-meaning priest was at the wrong bed, thank God.

As the days turned to weeks, I was nursed back to health. I looked skeletal, having lost 3 stones, but at least I was alive. The doctors had removed my spleen, I had internal bleeding and 3 broken ribs. My parents had been called to my bedside several times after being told I was dying and at best they gave me a 50/50 chance of survival. Really, I should have died that hot summer's day but, by whatever grace of God, I pulled through.

Upon eventually being discharged I was told that my injuries would prevent me from any pastimes that were deemed a contact sport. They also said that, having no spleen, I was at constant risk of catching even a common cold and advised that I should take antibiotics for the rest of my life.

I never took either piece of advice but, to this day I thank my Guardian Angel for sparing me, and the great team at the West Cumberland Hospital that had put me back together. My scooter was as equally broken as I was, but my old man spent every spare moment bringing it back to life.

My recuperation was to prove a long road. It was months before I began to feel somewhat like the old me. But, that first time back on my scooter felt amazing. My Mum later told me that the owner of the wall that I had smashed had phoned her demanding payment for the damage. The only damage they should have worried about was my old lady going around there for a 'polite word'. Suffice to say, they didn't pursue their claim. Talking of claims, some 6 months later the van driver settled out of court and paid me a meagre £1,000 for my suffering. The money faded as fast as the Doctor's advice, and I was soon back to being broke both financially and now physically.

I had been lucky. Okay, I was now without a spleen and my body was a bit battered, but at least I was alive. Death doesn't care if you are young or old, fat, thin, black or white. If you are caught in the Grim Reaper's crosshairs and your number is called, then that, unfortunately, is the cue for the fat lady to sing. There is never an easy time to lose anyone, but when a life is cut short it magnifies the tragedy and makes you question the meaning of life.

Up until this point I had only seen people die that had lived a long and happy life. My grandparents were into their 80's when they took their last breath. And, although it is sad, you can reason it, understand it and accept it. The first time I experienced the loss of someone that had their whole life ahead of them really knocked the stuffing out of me.

Only The Good Die Young

I had been at a mates' 18th Birthday 'do' in a rough Working Men's club in the coastal town of Whitehaven. The night was going well until a brawl broke out between the Mods and the local 'great unwashed'.

I ended up face down with two bouncers kicking the crap out of me. My mates had fared equally badly, and we were forced to beat a hasty retreat to the car park. We were royally outnumbered and these knobheads were a good few years older than us. We gave them a good go but, this was not our night and we were left bloodied and beaten. I was having trouble breathing through a broken nose and just wanted to go home.

My mate Paul hadn't been involved in the fight and, when we got onto our scooters, he said, "Let's go for a ride out to North Side and look at the sea."

Usually, I would have gone, but something made me say, "No, I'm heading home mate, my nose is fucked."

I waved as we headed in opposite directions, seeing Paul's tail-light disappear in the dark through my mirrors, little knowing it would be the last time I would see my friend alive.

The knock on my door the next day was a familiar sound. I knew it was the Police before my Dad had even answered the door. In my mind I thought they were here to lift me for the previous night's fight. How I wish it was so. My Dad called me into the living room.

"Gary, you need to sit down," he said, as I emerged from my bedroom.

"Paul is dead, and as you were with him last night, they want to talk to you."

I felt my legs go from under me. The officer told me that Paul's body had been found at the foot of the cliffs at North Side. They asked if I had gone too and, witnessing the accident, panicked and ran. My old man decided he didn't like the line of questioning and told the coppers to leave before he threw them out.

I was crushed. Paul was only 17 years old; this couldn't be happening. The verdict of *death by misadventure* was later recorded by the coroner. The funeral cortege was led by 70 scooters, all there to pay their respect to their lost brother. Paul was laid to rest in a purple mohair suit he recently had made to measure.

His parents never got over his death. The headlines that drew a comparison to the end sequence in the Mod film Quadrophenia did not help them either. Paul was destined never to grow old, his life cut short before his promise could be met. I often recall my final memory as he rode into the darkness never to see the light again.

My head was battered. I spiralled into a self-destructive mess, self-medicating to block out the guilt I felt. I should have gone with him, maybe I could have stopped the accident. The scene of Paul's death was a dark road. The coroner and Police said that he had rode to close to the edge before plummeting over the 40-foot drop.

13

The First Cut Is The Deepest

"Life is a drink, and you get drunk when you're young."
Paul Weller

When you are young, death and mortality are not at the forefront of your mind. And, although my crash and Paul's death had shaken me and, at the time, made me more aware of the thin veil that separates this world and the next, I still thought, deep down, that I was invincible.

This is a curse of the young. We took chances, put ourselves into situations that were dangerous and generally walked around in a blinkered ignorance. Youth and danger come together like iron filings and a magnet. So, it was no surprise that I was soon back to playing another game of chance with the Grim Reaper.

Knives and weapons were less apparent back then, or so it seemed. I had a couple of close calls with 'sharps' and, no matter what anyone tells you in a self-defence class, when you are staring at the business end of a blade, all the techniques you have drilled go South (usually leaving a yellow trail running down your inside leg).

The first time I was cut was at school. I had gotten into an argument with a lad called Bobby Williams. He was the 'cock' of our year and, generally, we got on okay. Only this time, I was in his crosshairs and he wanted to make a statement after I had bettered him in a friendly fight. Egos and youth, a lethal combination.

Long story short, he pulled a Stanley knife on me and, as I tried to block the attack, my hand was cut open quite deeply. The sight of the blood spurting out seemed to set Bobby into a panic and he took to his heels. I never told any teachers, as being labelled a 'grass' was the worst thing that could happen in a school like mine. Bobby later apologised, and we got over our spat.

Some years later I was again looking down the business end of a knife. I had gotten into one of those stupid arguments that teenagers attract. This one started in the usual feeling-out way, "What you lookin' at?"

I didn't really have an answer as I was completely thrown off guard. We were standing at a bus stop, there really wasn't much to look at other than what was in front of you, so this lad might have had a point (no pun intended). He was an ugly-looking git too, so my response, "Fuck knows," went down like a lead balloon.

The next thing that happened made my stomach lurch into a somersault that would have made an Olympic gymnast proud. Beads of sweat broke out on my forehead and I'm sure my mouth must have fallen open in total shock. The blade was small but, make no mistake, it would still make a mess of me had it gotten the chance to penetrate my body. This clown was waving the knife around like some stereotypical leather-clad baddie from a B-movie.

The long-awaited bus pulled up and, as its doors swung open, I had a moment to make my move. Yes, I should have run, but that's not how it went down. The knife was being passed from left to right, I knew I had to make a definitive statement if I was to walk away unscathed.

Bang. My right fist connected with the ugly fuck's jaw. He staggered back, his calf catching the step of the bus and causing him to topple backwards. The blade had dropped from his hand and was now out of reach. I dived forward, straddling the now prone attacker, and went to work punching his bouncing head until I was sure he was out of the game. The passengers on the bus must have been in shock as a few screams brought me back to reality, and I stopped dead in my tracks.

I decided that asking the driver for a ticket and finding a seat was not in my best interests, so I jumped off the bus and ran until exhausted and safely away from the scene of the crime. I knew it was self-defence, but I also knew that the local constabulary had a rather thick file with my name on it. I was shaking like a shitting dog but, at the same time, elated to have laid the horrible fucker out. Maybe in future he would think twice about starting trouble for no reason. I hoped he was so fucked up that his parents would have to identify him by his dental records.

I certainly wasn't going to lose any sleep over him.

Buses must have been unlucky for me as the next time I was facing a sharp pointed object I was again aboard one. Only this time I was not alone. It was a work *pub crawl* and me and my mate, Moggy, were heading to the meet-up point on the good old Number 30.

We attracted a few odd looks as we boarded the packed bus. Moggy was dressed as Cooperman (a parody of Tommy Cooper dressed as Superman), complete with flowing red cape and wearing his underpants on the outside of his tights. I was dressed as Andy Pandy, the childhood hero of the 5 to 8-year-old population of 1970's Great Britain.

The work's do wasn't fancy dress, but we decided it would need a bit of livening up and a bit of a laugh. We took our seats and were happily talking and having a laugh, minding our own business. Opposite us sat a group of older men, probably in their early thirties (ancient). They had given us a look when we sat down, but we weren't aware that there would be any trouble.

One of the group was saying in a loud voice that Denis Law was the greatest footballer of all time. I was never really into football and turned to Moggy to ask, "Dennis Lawler? Who's he?"

Now, the unwritten law is that you should never argue about religion or politics, so I was most surprised when this bloke turned on me saying, "Shut your fucking mouth, you knobhead, or I'll shut it for you. It's Law, not Lawler."

I should have ignored the pillock but, that was something I had trouble doing.

"How, are you going to shut my mouth, Dickhead?"

At that, the aggrieved football fan and chairman of the Denis Law Fan Club got up and put his finger in my face.

"Fucking Andy Pandy? What a tool."

I stood up and said, "Let's have it then."

Moggy was trying to calm the situation as he knew that I was about to go off like a match in a firework factory. The Denis Law Appreciation Society stepped back and, reaching into his pocket, pulled out a set of darts.

"What the fuck are you going to do with those, you prick?" I laughed.

What an absurd situation. Here I was squaring-up, dressed as Andy Pandy, to a bloke now waving his favourite tungsten dart at me.

"Come on then, Jocky Wilson (former World Darts Champion), let's see if you can get a 180?"

I probably never said that line, but how I wish I had. I didn't wait for his reply, hitting him with a left and right combination that saw him and his darts toppling backwards. The bus screeched to a halt and the driver was shouting that he was going to drive to the Police station if we didn't get off the bus. At that, me and Cooperman decided to leg it.

After a good twenty minutes or so, a distant siren warned that the Old Bill were on our trail. Again, we took off, Moggy's cape billowing behind him as he nearly broke the land speed record for the two-minute mile. We managed to evade our pursuers with some nifty footwork. Afterwards, and after ditching our costumes, we laughed as we recounted the tale.

I would have loved to have heard the police radio, "We are in pursuit of Cooperman and Andy Pandy. Andy Pandy has knocked out a dart player on the Number 30." Happy days. I still smile when recalling this incident. The wanted posters would have been hilarious.

The Cooperman/Andy Pandy story makes light of the situation but, in all seriousness, contemplating trying to take a knife from someone is, by and large, the wrong decision. Run, and don't stop running until you have put a safe distance between you and the scumbag carrying the knife. Sometimes beating a hasty retreat is difficult. What if you are backed into a corner, or you are injured and unable to *have it away*? My advice is to pick up anything close to hand to use as a likely weapon.

I have lost count of the stupid advice and practical applications that so-called Martial Arts Masters have given for 'disarming' knives, guns, and any other makeshift weapon. Some of these idiots should be locked up for potentially endangering the lives of their students. I wouldn't even trust their hand to hand combat skills.

Unfortunately, the general public buy into the bullshit that these cowboys sell them. I once saw a fat American 'Master' teach a knife disarm which literally could have led to the person using the technique to lose a limb. His advice, when confronted by a blade was, and I quote, "Grab the blade, and at the same time strike the attacker in the face."

Seriously? Grab the blade? Take the advice but it's probably not going to help your future career if you want to be a concert pianist. It's the same with these idiots that believe that a Martial Art that was practical in feudal Japan will also be practical in the takeaway on a Saturday night when you knock some Neanderthal's kebab out of their hands.

You see it all the time. Attacker throws a punch, defender blocks and does up to five counters while the attacker stands like a mannequin, arm still outstretched until he is put down and the attack nullified. In Japan, during the time of the Samurai warrior, heavy armour made the movements slower, catching the arm was easier as a result, and the defences used might have had more chance. Although, if some pissed-off Samurai is swinging a heavy sword in my direction, I'm going to do like the shepherd does and get the flock out of there.

If you want to learn to defend yourself, learn an *alive* martial art. By that, I mean a martial art that you *pressure test* through sparring and not just drill over and over against a compliant partner. Anyway, that's my advice and it's the advice I would have shared with the exuberant youth that I was in that previous life. An awareness of impending danger and risk are your best defensive weapons. As great Martial strategist Sun Tzu once said, "Know thy enemy."

14

Hellhounds On My Trail

"We are each our own devil, and we make this world our Hell."
Oscar Wilde

As the 80's bows out, heralding in a new decade, the world is anything but settled. 1990 sees the allied troops being drafted into Iran following an invasion by moustachioed despot Saddam Hussein. Back in good old Blighty, the Tory Party decides to introduce a tax that causes riots and leads to the criminalisation of working-class objectors who refuse to pay. And, in better news, the figurehead of Yuppie Britain, Maggie Thatcher, stands down as Prime Minister, leaving successor John Major on hands and knees picking up the pieces of a battered and broken (Great)Britain.

The years melded into each other and, before I knew it, I could no longer blame my escapades on youthful exuberance. I was now into my 26th summer, I had a son, and a mortgage.

The *respectability vampire* had crept up behind me and sunk its fangs into my neck before I had even seen its approach. But, try as I might, walking away from trouble still felt impossible. I knew deep down that I was self-destructive to the point that all my relationships began to falter.

Friends I had stood back-to-back with now turned their backs and walked away. My relationship with Joan was suffering too. After all, who wants to be around someone that fights every weekend? Someone regularly coming home with the shirt ripped from their back, bleeding, ranting, and unable to hear the good sense that was being given by those that truly cared.

The truth was that I had been living this way for as long as I could remember. Even I didn't know why I was acting like this, or even what I was fighting for anymore. People knew me and knew how to push my buttons, or at least that's what I believed. Basically, I was apportioning blame to anyone but myself. I had suffered all my life with the unpredictability of my moods.

Friends would say they never knew which Gary would show up to the party. I could be bouncing off the walls one minute, and on the floor the next. The constant shifts in moods must have been so hard to deal with, and I certainly wouldn't stay with a Jekyll and Hyde character like me, so I couldn't really blame Joan when she called time on our relationship.

I had, in some respects, let myself go. Given up. I didn't really understand her reasoning at the time, but I do now. I gave her no choice. I pushed her, and everyone else, away. I was unable to function in a normal environment, partly because I didn't feel normal or even know what normal was. I was a square peg trying to fit into a round hole. I loved my son with all my heart but playing house and doing the things a Father and loving partner should do felt at odds to me. Joan wanted someone that could be sensible and committed.

I didn't deal with the break-up well. Alcohol became my doctor, my medicine and counsellor all rolled into one. I thought it was helping me to come to terms with my situation.

I moved into a flat that was strategically placed opposite my local pub. It didn't help that I also had a bank account that was flush from Joan buying me out of the house we had bought. It's scary how quickly £9,000 can disappear behind a bar. I was drinking morning, noon and most nights and it wasn't long before I had lost my job to go along with my Family and self-respect. The handful of friends I still had left were worried that I was going so far down I wouldn't or, more accurately, couldn't get back up. I went from 15 stone to 11 stone in a matter of months. It was as if I was committing a slow but sure suicide.

I was lost. My own worst enemy, unable or unwilling to help myself. The once-proud Mod now gave little thought to his appearance. I lived to drink and the drink, at least for a while, delivered a fog through which my problems looked less serious.

Throughout this time, I still had access to my son Jason, and on those days with him I had enough resolve not to drink. I didn't need it on those days, I was responsible for this child and nothing would stop me looking after him properly. It was the times I was alone that were the worst. I didn't like myself, let alone anyone else liking me and, at least when I was propping up the bar, I had people around me who, for as long as I bought the drinks, seemed to care. It's funny how quickly these so-called friends ran out as quickly as the money did.

The battle with drink was to prove a hard and dirty fight, and it was a fight that I was losing every day. I couldn't see it at the time, but I was wallowing in self-pity. I was self-destructing. In reality, I was a selfish idiot that had thrown away all the good things in my life, and that is a sad truth that I must live with. The only constant was the trouble that often goes hand in hand with a drink problem. I was a *social hand grenade*, pull the pin and watch me explode. I was always one drink away from causing myself or some other poor soul a world of pain. I started to see myself as a defender of people, getting involved in fights that were none of my business.

One night, when I stepped in front of some idiot that, to me, looked like he was going to put a glass in my best mates' face, I nearly ended up without my thumb.

Frank had been talking to a girl in the bar we were having a bevy in. Unbeknown to Frank, she wasn't alone. Her bloke was at the bar and, when he came back, he was less than impressed at the sight of his lady friend talking to this six-foot three skinhead. I saw him out of the corner of my eye and when I saw him pick up an empty glass, I was in no doubt about his intention. I didn't have time to warn Frank, who was more than capable of taking the glass from this poor sap and making him eat it. A nice right hand dropped the lad where he stood. The glass smashed onto the floor and from nowhere a couple of door lads came charging through the crowd. They stopped dead in their tracks when they caught sight of Frank and me, and after weighing things up picked the lad up and carried him outside.

It was nearly chucking-out time anyway, so it wasn't long after that we also left the bar. Surprisingly, the lad I had decked was waiting, albeit a bit bloody. His lady friend was begging him to walk away but he wasn't for listening. He rushed at me, arms flailing. I managed to use his momentum and throw him to the cold pavement. I was on top now and determined to make him pay. One hand was on his throat choking him, the other was balled-up and smashing into his face. I went to work on him like a demented sculptor.

I'm not sure if it was in panic or if he was just trying to survive by any means, but he managed to get my thumb into his mouth and was attempting to bite right through. The pain was unbelievable. I could feel skin being torn away as he set his jaw down. I needed to think fast.

Putting my other thumb into his eye socket was the only way that I could think of to make him release his grip on my now nearly-severed thumb. I pushed deep into his eye, if I was losing a thumb, he was going to lose an eye. Brutal, I know, but when the chips are down it really is a dog eat dog world, so to speak.

The thumb in his eye had the desired effect and he released his bite. I finished him off with elbows, leaving him a bloody and battered mess. Frank grabbed me, and we ran. My thumb needed sewing up, so our first port of call was the hospital. Another battle wound, but more importantly a lesson learned.

I had the usual next-day panic, but it was only a fleeting thing, as every time I looked at my badly scarred and grotesquely swollen thumb, all pity washed away. It was like all the violent situations, the day after you are full of good intentions to change your ways, "I will be one of those people that can walk away. I have nothing to prove."

But, alas, reality can hit you like a train and the next time you find yourself face to face with another person intent on knocking you out, morals go out of the window, replaced with that most human need, survival. In my experience, walking away only gave these people an advantage. Most of the people I had stood toe to toe with didn't give a fuck for fair play. They wanted an easy target.

I was never going to give them the satisfaction.

15

I Fought the Law (but the Law won)

"If you don't know where you are going, any road will take you there." George Harrison

I was awaiting trial after a fight in which one of the group of lads that had jumped me ended up with a broken leg. I might have got away with it, had it not been for the Police interview.

"How come, if you were the one jumped by three lads, the only injury was to this fella's leg?"

Stupidly, and looking back my answer was probably fuelled by ego and alcohol, a lethal combination, I gave the answer that nearly cost me my liberty right then and there. And under caution.

"I know Karate."

Boom. I might as well have just announced that the entire police department had won on their collective spot-the-ball or pools entry (for the younger reader, the pools and spot-the-ball were our Lottery tickets back in the day). It wasn't my first offence either, I was well known to the police as a brawler.

I decided that in Court I would plead *not guilty*. The Law really doesn't like this approach, especially when a group of working-class lads have been locking horns outside a pub in a respectable area. Usually the same part of town that houses the magistrates that hold your balls in their hands.

Magistrates have always been something of an enigma to me. Usually they are working class people that have moved up the social ladder with a foot firmly placed on the middle class rung. They have no training in Law and are directed in their decisions and outcomes by the Clerk of the Court. The image I hold to this day of the lesser-spotted Magistrate is that of social climber, a suited and booted, morally irreproachable person looking over half-moon glasses in bemused disgust at the *oik* brought before them. A delinquent piece of shit that they see as a threat to their cosy new world order. Someone to scoff over with their significant other half as they drink a glass of civilised red wine with their dinner.

Their real thrill is to be safe in the knowledge that they are 'doing their bit for society'. Keeping the scum where they belong, in a subservient stoop, tugging at their forelock and begging leniency for being born on the wrong side of the track.

I have seen many good people that were just in the wrong place at the wrong time criminalised by overzealous policing and later suffering harsh penalties that were handed down by the fine and upright citizens that feel the need to judge others. Anyway, I digress.

By whatever stroke of luck, I didn't get sent down, but the fine imposed and the warning that this was my last chance really hit home. That, and the week's headline in the local paper, "Karate Expert in Brawl", or words to that effect.

I knew that I had to change. I was a Father, and besides, I was too pretty to go to jail. Alcohol is a cruel mistress. If I was to sort my life out, I had to admit that I had a problem. It wasn't just drink with me though, I had a serious mental health condition that, coupled with drink, magnified my problems tenfold.

At this time, I didn't realise I was unwell. I put my behaviour down to many things. I was excusing my behaviour on anything and everything. The drink wasn't the real issue. The real issue was the fact that I was self-medicating.

The violence was getting out of hand. I was upping the level of aggression with each conflict. I really didn't care what happened, either to me or the poor sap on the receiving end of my anger.

This was brought home to me one night, travelling as a passenger in a car. The driver, Richard, who was a mate of my brother, had been winding me up all night. When he couldn't get a reaction, he upped the ante, talking about my brother and how he was going to make a move on his Mrs. And when that failed to piss me off, he said, "I might go and set fire to his house."

This was some sick and twisted stuff. My niece was only 6 months old, so the thought of him carrying out his threat sent me into a meltdown. From my position on the back seat I couldn't get a good punch off, so I grabbed his seat belt and pulled it tightly across his throat. The car was careering across the road which, luckily as it was late, was empty. I could hear the fucker choking, but still I pulled the makeshift noose tighter.

"Pull over!" I shouted, releasing the grip just enough to keep him from passing out.

The car swerved, skidded and came to a violent stop. The force sent me forward and I made a sudden impact with the seat in front. Richard slumped, his head laying on the steering wheel. I jumped out of the car and, wrenching open the driver side door, made a grab for the sick bastard. I had his throat in one hand as the other curled into a fist that connected with his now bloody face time and again.

It should have been enough, but I was still in the midst of an anger that showed no sign of dissipating. The red mist had taken hold like a 1970's wrestler locking on a Full Nelson. I dragged his half-conscious body out of the car and, holding the door with one hand, moved his head into the gap between the door and the car. I gave it several slams, until his now-limp body slumped to the cold ground.

My senses jump-started back to life and I took to my heels. I spent a long night waiting for the Police, but as the sun broke through the darkness and my door was still on its hinges, I started to worry that maybe I had gone too far. What if I had killed him? The phone broke the spell and brought me back to my senses. The familiar voice of my sister in law asked me what had I done to Richard?

"Is he okay?" I offered weakly.

"He looks like he's been run over by a truck. What the fuck happened? He won't tell us anything other than you went mad and attacked him," she countered.

"I'll come and see you, I want him to tell you himself," I said.

By the time I had got to my brother's house, Richard had left. Not only my brother's house, but his own place too. He had *done a runner*. He told my brother that if I ever went near him again, he would get the police to arrest me.

My family were convinced that I had just lost the plot and attacked Richard for nothing, my protestations falling on deaf ears.

Even my parents looked at me as if I was an animal. I was told that I had issues, that I was dangerous and needed to get help. I genuinely started to feel ill. I couldn't make anyone listen to me.

My frustration boiled over and, in a fit of temper, I started punching doors, walls and anything else that came into my view. Soon the house was turned upside down. But still I couldn't stop. Something in me had snapped, I was running amok, destroying anything in my path, a human tornado.

When at last I collapsed exhausted, the chaos subsiding, I knew I had gone too far. A Doctor arrived. I'm not sure where he came from but, after speaking to my parents, he said that he was going to give me something to calm me down. I went along with it as I didn't have the energy to argue. If I had refused, I think I would have been sectioned.

I don't recall what he injected me with, but I soon drifted into a calm and peaceful sleep. There was talk about psychiatric help, but nothing ever happened. I was given pills. They were supposed to keep me calm, and for a while they worked. But the pills were about as effective as a sticking plaster on a gaping wound.

It was at this low point that I started to look to my past and how the Martial Arts training in my youth was the happiest time of my life. If I carried on living the way I had for more years than I cared to remember then, at best, I was looking at a prison sentence and at worst an early grave. Shamefully, I had turned my back on the one thing in my life that had given me a sense of belonging, the Martial Arts.

I didn't care for the person that woke each day, struggling to look at the grey shallow reflection that bounced back from the mirror. Being part of something like Modernism had filled a void, but it wasn't the way to stay away from trouble. Drinking only gave life to the demons that snapped at my heels. And, as much as I tried to fit in, I never really could. I had hit a wall, and the only way was either through it, over it, or accept it as my destiny. Maybe my decision to change and return to some form of combat training wouldn't win the war that I was waging against myself, but it might just prove a small victory.

16

The Man Who Fell To Earth

"Doh!" Homer Simpson

I thought long and hard about returning to Karate but, in all the fights I had been in, I could honestly say that I was unable to use the techniques I had learned to any great effect.

The one time I tried to use pure Karate techniques in a *straightener* I came close to receiving the biggest beating of my life (although, on reflection, it wasn't Karate that let me down but my own stupidity).

I had gotten into an argument with a lad I vaguely knew. The usual pushing and goading escalated into a challenge to sort it out on the football field at 5.00pm the next night. I can't remember why we didn't just fight there and then, but we didn't. Anyone that tells you that they are not nervous in a situation like this is lying. The build up to the fight saw me running through every scenario possible, from me knocking this idiot out with one punch, to me being sparked by him with one punch.

The news of the fight had spread and there was going to be a big crowd watching and baying for their pound of flesh the next day. I think I was more frightened of losing in front of my mates than the person I was fighting. After all, I knew Karate.

I decided, stupidly, to have a little bit of insurance as I had heard that this lad liked to fight dirty. Unfortunately, my insurance policy proved to be my downfall, quite literally. I wore a pair of football boots, minus the studs. I didn't want to get called a cheat when I finished the fight with a well-timed kick to my opponent's head.

The fight started in the usual way; a bit of pushing before the first punch was thrown. I got off well with a nice right hand that caught my opponent clean on the nose. First blood, me. From there, things went from bad to worse. I launched a roundhouse kick at his head, only to find myself sailing through the air having slipped on my non-grip footwear.

Bang. He didn't waste any time and booted me hard in the face. Not once or twice, but ten or fifteen kicks hit me. I tried in vain to regain my footing, but every time I did, I slipped again like a silent movie star stepping on a banana skin.

Soon, his unrelenting kicks had opened cuts and closed both of my eyes. I was being mauled, but something made me get up, time and again. Pride or stupidity, it didn't matter which, as I was facing a beating under the glare of my watching mates. In the end, someone jumped in and separated us. I didn't see who as my eyes were completely shut and I was bleeding profusely.

Worse than the physical pain was the thought that I had been beaten in front of my friends. The same friends that I had been boasting to about my Karate prowess. And, although people were happily saying it was a draw as no one had given up, I knew I was beaten. And worse, I was beaten by my own stupidity.

People often say that life teaches us our most valuable lessons. I certainly learned that day that I was not the master technician I thought I was. I was just like everybody else, scared and unsure in times of violent confrontation. I had had the living crap kicked out of me and, long after the bruising and swelling had gone, the dent to my fragile ego remained.

You could argue that my choice of footwear beat me that day, but I believe it was the greatest example of pride coming before a fall, and I can honestly say, in hindsight, that I deserved that beating and more, and that I am glad it happened. I now realise that it isn't the Martial Art that's at fault, rather the way we train.

I know, and am fortunate to know, some truly amazing Karate Ka, people I have trained with and some I have witnessed using Karate to great effect. Martial Arts offer so much more than just a way to kick the crap out of someone, the discipline and confidence you get from training is invaluable. But I still believe that any Martial Art or combat system has limitations and to a degree there is always a need to look outside the confines of your system. I just wasn't ready to fully understand this yet, but with time and experience comes wisdom. Unfortunately, sometimes we must learn the hard way, and our greatest lesson can come from our most crushing defeat.

Anyway, Karate didn't hold the same interest for me that it once had. I found a Japanese Jujitsu school not far from my home and decided to check it out. This was perhaps the greatest development in my Martial Arts journey and the most significant discovery of a pure fighting system that I had made up to this point.

My first visit to the jujitsu school didn't quite go to plan. I got to the venue early and waited. After about 20 minutes past the time that the class was due to start, another student turned up. He tried the locked door, mumbled something, and then turned and walked away. It seemed that this school was a bit *hit and miss* as to whether it bothered to open.

The next scheduled training session I was pleased to see the doors open and could hear a few voices coming from inside. A better start than my previous attempt to join the jujitsu class. I am not sure if it was because the class was being held in a school and it brought back bad memories, or maybe it was because it was the fear of the unknown, but I was absolutely *bricking it* as I entered the hall.

It wasn't particularly busy, perhaps six people in total. The uniforms were the first thing that intrigued me. I was not used to seeing Martial Arts practiced in light blue cotton uniforms with red stripes going down the arms and legs. I quite liked it. It reminded me of those funky yellow Karate suits that the competitors on Han's Island had worn in Enter the Dragon.

But this was no Bruce Lee movie. I reminded myself that we were in a school hall and I was about to be introduced to the gentle art of Japanese Jujitsu. That was the second revelation. If this was gentle, God help me. I got more bruises and injured limbs in that first session than I got in all my collective years as a Karateka.

I loved it. It was as if I had glimpsed Nirvana. I felt a sense of belonging straight away and couldn't wait for the next lesson. Strangely, the nervous feeling that I experienced on that very first session never went away. The walk up the path to the training hall felt like I was walking the Green Mile. For a traditional Martial Art, this style of jujitsu was very eclectic in its approach. We learned how to box, used Muay Thai kicks and knees, and did a lot of Randori (rolling).

It was always the ground fighting that intrigued me the most. The head coach was a good grappler and, in my opinion, was way ahead of the game. Bear in mind that this was long before we had heard about BJJ, or the UFC for that matter.

The three lessons each week soon became the highlights of my week. I would dash home from work, shower and head to the session. I later started doing a weekly private session with the head coach. These private sessions usually entailed ten minutes of technique followed by fifty minutes of sparring, starting on the feet wearing gloves and ending on the floor, rolling for submissions. It was not uncommon for me to leave the session injured and limping but, as hard as it was, I wouldn't quit. If the saying that *iron sharpens iron* is true, then this environment became my foundry. The training was brutal, with beginners unable to survive the warm-ups, let alone the main training regime.

I was a green belt at the time of my first competition. We had joined the NJJKC and they had formulated a set of rules for their Kumite competition. In short, you could kick, punch and grapple to submission. The ideal way to test our training.

I was really looking forward to competing under these rules as they favoured my aggressive style. The competition was in the Midlands, and we travelled down on the morning of the comp, arriving with minutes to spare.

My first fight went to plan. I scored with a high roundhouse kick to the head and followed up with a hard body shot. I felt the air leave my opponent's body like a punctured ball and he dropped to his knees. I knew that any fight he had in him had gone. He didn't want it anymore.

Desperate to make up the lost points and save face, he tried one last-ditch attempt to take me down with a throw, but I thwarted all attacks and went on to win the bout with ease.

My second fight went the same way and, with another win under my belt, my confidence was growing. Now, confidence is a great trait in any sport, but overconfidence is not, and I was about to learn this the hard way. My next opponent was taller than me - not hard at my five foot eight inches without the 1970's platform shoes. This guy was well over six feet tall with the sort of frame that favoured a kicker with his long legs. And he was fast with it. So fast, in fact, that I didn't even see the kick that hit me flush on the temple or even realise I had been caught until I was flat on my back, looking up at the ceiling. I could hear my teammates shouting, "Stay down! Recover!" and that was great advice, had I bothered to take it.

I was given some time to shake off the KO, but for some reason I jumped up and launched, rather wobbly, at my opponent, anger now coursing through me.

Boom. Straight into another hard shot. I was picked off at will after that and lost the fight on points. I got to fight for the Bronze medal and won, which for my first comp I should have been over the moon about. I wasn't. I went home feeling disappointed that I had let myself and my team down. I was determined that this would never happen again. I knew that I could have won Gold that day.

I also knew that my fitness had let me down even though I had trained hard. And then there was the fact that I had seen red and lost control of myself. Anger is never good in a combat situation, it clouds your judgement, slows your reactions and makes you react in the wrong way.

After the loss, I totally dedicated myself to training. I started running in the morning before work, slowly building up my stamina until I could run 5 miles without too much effort. The jujitsu training was stepped up and, instead of training 4 times a week, I made sure I was training every day, without excuse. I became absorbed in the practice of Martial Arts again and it was all I could think about day in and day out. A long shift at the factory didn't feel so bad after my morning run and training to look forward to after work. I had a purpose and wanted to compete as often as I could, I needed to prove to myself that I could win a big competition and not only win but win in style.

My time to shine came sooner than I had anticipated. The North of England Jiu-Jitsu Kumite Championships were to be held in Carlisle in a couple of months' time. I would be ready.

My training comprised of endless rounds against a fresh opponent, what I now know to be called 'shark tanking'. Rounds would be 5 minutes long or until someone tapped-out. For the person in the middle, the bait, a new and fresh opponent would just launch themselves at you, which often meant they started on your back trying to choke the life out of you. These sessions were brutal and after you had finished your turn in the tank you would literally crawl off the mats, leaving a trail of sweat and, often, blood behind you. Drilling techniques was also a prerequisite of the training camp. I would perform countless *guillotine* and other high percentage submissions until they became second nature.

The day of the championships finally arrived. There were a lot of people in my category, and it meant multiple fights to get to the final. I was fit enough and had confidence (but not too much) in my abilities to come out on top, whether it was a stand up or ground fighting scenario. I breezed past my first few opponents, using my reliable and much-tested roundhouse kick to score first. If it went to the ground, I handled myself well enough to *reverse* and *submit* my opponent.

I eventually made it to the final. Nothing was going to stop me now, that Gold and, more to the point the title, was going to be mine. This was my day. I couldn't imagine that anyone had trained as hard as me or been on the receiving end of the beatings dished out to me daily over the past few months. The competition was the easy part, the hard part was behind me, for now. Sometimes everything just falls into place, it is your time, and you just feel untouchable, like time is moving in slow motion. This was one of those days.

I stepped onto the mat. I could hear my coach and teammates in the background, but I was as focused as I had ever been in my life. My opponent was good, I wouldn't have wanted it any other way. He scored first and hard with a sidekick to my stomach. I remained calm. The sound of my instep bouncing off his head was satisfying and meant that I was taking control. I got the takedown and mounted for what seemed like a lifetime. This guy was bucking harder than a wild stallion to get me off.

The referee stood us back up due to inactivity. It wasn't that I wasn't trying to submit my opponent, his defence was just too good. We danced around each other, feinting with jabs, or lifting the lead foot to find an opening. He moved into me. My timing was impeccable as my foot snaked through his defences and connected solidly with his jaw. Not waiting for him to fall from the power of the kick, I *lit him up* with a back fist and reverse punch to the mid-section. Game over.

I had won the North of England Jiu-Jitsu Kumite title. I shook hands with my opponent who promised to beat me in the Nationals later that year. But I didn't care, I had proven that hard work pays off, a mantra that was to stay with me throughout my competitive career.

After 8 years of training in Japanese Jujitsu I was told that I would be grading for my black belt. The test was two hours long and involved demonstrations of self defence techniques and sparring. I had been preparing for this test for a long time and was confident in my abilities. The morning of the exam soon came around and as I walked onto the tatami my coach called me over and said, "I'm going to break your arm."

He was trying to get inside my head, and although I was nervous, I didn't give it too much thought, it was just a part of the grading, his subtle way of trying to psyche me out, at least that's what I hoped. After an hour of demonstrating the syllabus techniques, I was told to prepare for sparring. I was given a pair of MMA gloves and told that I would be fighting a fresh opponent at the end of each round. I knew that this was the real 'test'. There was no protective equipment other than the 4-ounce gloves, full power was the order of the day. If you were knocked out or injured you were given the option of quitting and coming back another day to try again. There was no way I was going to give up and, as my first opponent took his place opposite me, I felt confident that I could come through this ordeal. We had done a lot of sparring in the past so I knew that I was as ready as I could be. I was fit and strong and could take a good punch. Each round was at least 5 minutes long but occasionally, even after the timer had sounded, the call came from the grading panel to continue. After what seemed like the longest day of my life, but was in fact only an hour of non-stop sparring, I was told to get some water. But if I thought that this was the end of the grading I was mistaken, as the head coach, the man that had previously told me he would break my arm, stepped up. I had sparred with this man many times, and as my skills had grown I had given him some good, hard fights. Only now, soaked in sweat, my arms and legs feeling like lead and my face battered and bloody, I knew that this was going to be make or break time. We both took up our stances and prepared to knock some serious lumps out of each other. I was hit with a hard right hand that rocked me but didn't put me down. I launched at my opponent and took the fight to the ground where I attempted a few punches. Some got through but I soon found myself reversed and being pummelled. My instructor could probably have finished the fight there and then, but he really wanted a stand up fight, so he backed up and shouted for me to 'get the fuck up'. I struggled but managed to lift my beaten and exhausted body off the bloodstained mats. Once upright, I was aware of my laboured breathing and, worryingly, my sight that was starting to fail. It didn't help that there were rivulets of sweat running into my eyes, or that my nose was broken. The other students were shouting for me to 'dig deep', but all I could do was try to survive this fight the best I could. I was straightened with a stiff jab and lit up with a hard roundhouse kick to my jaw. It rocked me but I was still in the game. I was being hit at will now, but noticed that the shouting had stopped to be replaced with an uneasy silence as if it had dawned on the students in attendance that this spectacle didn't make for easy viewing and, worse, they realised that their time would come if they stayed the course. My friend John, a recently promoted Black belt shouted from the sidelines, "He's had enough. Come on stop this." But that only seemed to reignite my coach's desire to finish me off. It felt as if a couple of my ribs had broken, but something stopped me from quitting. I launched at my coach, fists flying, some connecting, some finding air. I needed to slow him down, and with all the energy I could muster, I threw a hard roundhouse kick that should have found the ribcage but instead connected with his elbow. The pain shot through me like a thousand volts and I dropped to the floor.

"You want to call it a day, Sav?" offered my coach in a mocking tone. My mate John now stood up and again asked that the fight be stopped.

"No fucking chance," I retorted, stumbling towards my coach with all the grace of a drunken dance floor dad. I was snapped down, where I lay exhausted I didn't get chance to contemplate my next move as a thumping pain shot through my neck from the axe kick that finally put an end to my grading. My foot was broken, but apart from that I was alright. Nothing a long hot bath wouldn't sort out. I was awarded my Black belt that day and, in all honesty, I wouldn't have wanted it any other way. I thought that this was all there was, that I had found my Martial Art, Japanese Jujitsu.

And then a few weeks later, someone handed me a VHS tape and said, "Watch this."

The title didn't really mean that much at first look, but something about the picture on the cover and the words underneath struck a chord.

"There are no rules."

I put the tape into my VHS player that night not really knowing what to expect. Little did I know, but this piece of *celluloid gold*, "Ultimate Fighting Challenge 1" (UFC 1), was to change my life and my Martial arts destiny.

17

Start

"Sometimes our light goes out but is blown again into instant flame by an encounter with another human being." Albert Schweitzer

In November of 1993 in Denver, Colorado, a clean-cut Brazilian changed the history of Martial Arts forever when he won the first 'Ultimate Fighting Challenge'. In so doing, Royce Gracie awakened a sleeping giant that was to tear to shreds the idea that all Martial Arts were unbeatable and that those that claimed expertise in these arts had mystical powers.

All Aboard the Gracie Train

Shortly after I had seen the UFC tape, Rorion and Royce Gracie made a series of instructional videos called, imaginatively, "Gracie Jiu-Jitsu - Beginner to Intermediate".

I, like many others that had been affected positively by the UFC tape, paid my hard-earned dollar and waited patiently to learn the secrets of this great new Jiu-Jitsu system from Brazil. I theorised that it must be some kind of magic to allow a skinny kid to not only beat his much larger opponents, but also make all the other Martial Arts that were represented look stiff and ineffective. The VHS tapes eventually arrived, and I couldn't wait to load them into my video player.

I watched the entire series in one go, taking notes and trying to remember the moves so that I could try them out later, on my training partners. The first thing that struck me was that some of the moves were almost identical to the ones that I had learned in my traditional jujitsu training. There must be something that I was missing?

Leverage. I had heard talk of this feature of Brazilian Jiu-Jitsu that made it more effective and was the reason it was different from the traditional Japanese system. I must admit, I didn't understand what this term 'leverage' meant, let alone how to apply it. One thing that did impress me though, was how smooth Rorion and Royce were. The moves themselves, although not a million miles away from the stuff I already knew, just looked so effortless. It was beautiful to watch.

I wanted to get that level of fluidity and grace into my own application of the techniques. I made the decision to stop training my Japanese curriculum and spent hours drilling the handful of moves that were presented on the tapes. I had started teaching at my own place too, and with the help of my mate John we soon built up a good and loyal base of students. John liked the traditional side of the training, which meant that I could concentrate on sparring and rolling, a match made in heaven.

I wore the Gracie Jiu-Jitsu tapes out, but it didn't matter. Doing so meant that I knew the content inside-out. The effect that UFC 1 had on me cannot be emphasised enough. I couldn't understand why, after witnessing the greatest combative contest ever staged, that anybody would stay with the traditional systems. To my mind, discovering UFC 1 was akin to that first moment man had walked on the moon, the invention of flight, the wheel, and any other massive leap that had taken man from the cave to where we are today.

I felt sorry for the people that refused to acknowledge its importance. How could people be so blind to the singular and most important discovery in the history of the Martial Arts? After all, the UFC had answered that age-old question: what was the most effective style of fighting? UFC had not only answered it, it now posed serious questions about the validity of the traditional fighting arts.

To a martial artist looking for some truth amongst a history of uncertainty, this was the missing link.

18

A Town Called Malice

"Better stop dreaming of the quiet life, 'cause it's the one we'll never know." Paul Weller

Following the breakdown of my relationship with Joan, I secured a low-paid job in a small coastal town called Maryport or, as the locals called it, 'Scaryport'.

Maryport was insular. Everyone knew everyone else and most were related in some way. They were so close, in fact, that if you kicked one of them in the shin, they all limped. I had also started a relationship with a girl called Donna at the factory I was working in. After a few short months, we moved into a new home together and, 9 months or so later, we had a beautiful baby boy, Josh. A new start.

To supplement the meagre wages I was earning at the factory, I started working weekends as a DJ and Doorman in a rather rough establishment in the town. In those days there wasn't a licensed body (SIA) to oversee the working practices of frontline Door Staff. The only qualification needed was that you could at least handle yourself reasonably well in the event of a kick-off.

There were two of us. One would change the disc and give it a bit of patter, whilst the other, if needed, which was every week at some point, would escort one of the local idiots off the premises. It might not have been the best way to stay out of fights, but it was a great way to test the Jiu-Jitsu techniques that I was working on.

The pub had a bad reputation thanks to a gang of druggies that frequented the bar. Every week, this group of clowns would try and frighten off any respectable clientele. With no punters, they figured they had the run of the place. We had other ideas, which didn't exactly make us popular with these half-baked morons. But I wasn't overly concerned as I wasn't there to make friends.

Life became one long, adrenaline and booze-fuelled party of violence and mayhem. I became addicted to the weekly high of facing-off these drug-pushing petty criminals.

Every Saturday and Sunday would be the same shit just a different day. We would walk into the pub, set the sound system up, and wait. We weren't waiting for the night to start, we were waiting for the footfall of the drug gang coming up the stairs. They came in early every Saturday and Sunday, occupying the seats closest to the entrance. If new faces came in, they would harass them, making them feel so uncomfortable that they would invariably leave, never to return.

We had been warned about this group before taking on the job. The owner was at a loss as to why his business was failing although, if he had bothered to look closely, he would see that one of his sons was part of the druggie gang and was lauding it up with his cronies every week.

Our first night saw a pitched battle when I threw one of the idiots out for dancing on a tabletop. I guess his friends didn't like the fact that we stood up to them, because at closing they were refusing to leave. The odds weren't particularly good: two against ten or twelve drug-fuelled hyenas. Cowards of the highest order, they wouldn't fight fairly if their lives depended on it. If they thought that we would lay down and just take a beating, they were mistaken.

Even after they put us on the ground we kicked back, refusing to stay down and play dead. They eventually backed off to admire their handy work. What they didn't expect was me getting back to my feet, armed with a pool cue that I had made a grab for in the fracas. I swung it wildly around at heads, legs, and any other available target that was presented. It turned the odds a little in our favour, and when Gaz, my *oppo*, got back to his feet too, we were back in the fight. In fact, it was starting to look like we could win this one.

Eventually the cowards backed off, crowing and making threats that they would finish us the next night. We were bloody and bruised but what a feeling! The pub closed for the night and we stayed and had a well-deserved pint or five, flushed with pride and talking about the fight and how we had come out on top.

We might have won the battle, but the war was far from over. But that didn't matter, we were buzzing with the excitement. We had set out our stall and were ready for whatever this bunch of dimwits could throw at us, literally.

Sunday night saw us walk into a battle arena again. This time we were greeted with the goading and whistling of a somewhat larger group. It wasn't long into the night that the idiots started to try and wind us up again. If it was up to me, we would have banned them all after last night's fight but, because the owner was blinded by misplaced loyalty to his son, they were not dealt with in the proper way.

So, we had to do things the hard way. About an hour into our set, one of the goons decided to bait us. He moved away from the pack and sat opposite our booth, blowing kisses and flipping the middle finger whenever I caught his eye. Which was more and more often as the night went on. Eventually, I decided that enough was enough and, telling Gaz to watch my back, I walked over to the monkey-faced freak and asked him if he had a problem, other than the obvious one.

His grin further annoyed me and, before he could answer, I planted a rapid three or four shots into his ugly mug, causing him to topple to the floor like a building that had been raised to the ground. At this, his so-called mates gave up a cheer and laughed at their fallen comrade's demise.

I should have been surprised but, given that this lot had the combined IQ of your average village idiot, I wasn't. I dragged Mr Happy to his feet and launched him back towards his hapless friends, who by now had started to walk towards me in what they thought was a menacing manner. This time we were ready for their assault and brought out a couple of *equalisers* in the form of an old rounder's bat and *Ol' Faithful* from the night before, my personal weapon of choice, the pool cue.

They were under no illusion this time that we would use any means necessary to protect ourselves and, for once in their pathetic lives, made the right decision and retreated. What we didn't realise was that their retreat was tactical and that night after we had finished, we were ambushed as we were loading the van. This time we had no chance and were beaten quite badly. I made a mental note of the ring leaders and, even as I was staving off kicks and punches, I was already planning my revenge.

Once the swelling had gone down and the stitches were removed, I was ready to go. I got a phone call one morning to say that the leader of this gang, a local 'businessman', had been saying that he was going to kill me. A couple of times recently I had noticed a car

I didn't recognise slowly driving past, and on one occasion the driver made the sign of a gun with his hand and pointed it at my house.

My second born, Josh, was sleeping upstairs at the time, and the sight of this local gangster making a thinly-veiled threat to my family sent me over the edge. Next morning, I decided to confront the situation head on.

It was a quiet Sunday morning when I pulled up outside the pub that was run by the 'Don'. Banging on the door like a wild man, fuelled by a rage that consumed me completely, I gave little thought to any consequences. The door swung open and I was thrown by the sight of the cleaning lady.

"Where is he?" I shouted.

Over her shoulder I saw my target. He wasn't alone. Just behind him was his minder, the colossus that ran the door.

"Let's go!" I shouted, entering the bar area.

The door shut behind me and the cleaning lady, as if in a Wild West cowboy movie, hightailed it out the back. It was at this point I realised that I had played right into this man's hands. I stood, fists clenched ready.

"Just you and me!" I shouted.

In a strange way, I admired the way that they had trapped me. Sun Tzu was one of my favourite strategists and, having read *The Art of War* several times, I knew that I was out-manoeuvred. Backed into a corner. Ambushed.

Surprisingly, my foe (let's call him Tommy), adopted a Karate stance. His sidekick (no pun intended), let's call him 'Odd Job', was ushered to the side.

And then it was on.

I aimed a kick at Tommy's ample frame which knocked him backwards and over a metal-based table. I was quick to follow him and launched a mounted attack, punching him hard in the head. It was then that Odd Job intervened, pulling me off and holding me long enough for Tommy to get to his feet and compose himself.

I was hit with several good punches that dazed me but, possessed by rage and after shrugging Odd Job off me, I kept coming forward. Back and forth we went, the sound of knuckle bouncing off flesh, accompanied by a strange growling that emitted from my opponent as we exchanged blows.

He was good and had obviously taken some Karate training in between his day job as the local Don (more Desperate Don than Don Corleone though). His technique was as rough as sandpaper but, to be fair, no technique looks like it does in the dojo, and his was as much a bastardisation of all he had used in the street as it was taken from a Martial Arts curriculum. His punches were hard, using his hips to generate power, and he was aggressive with it. But the adrenaline was coursing through me like a bullet train on full tilt and I felt no more than a dull thud against my face. This was for real.

I caught Tommy with a hard right and followed it with a knee that bounced off his head, sending a reverberation around the empty bar. Tommy sprawled onto the beer-stained carpet. Again, I pounced, and again, his dance partner pulled me off, holding me tighter this time.

Instead of a punch upon recovery, Tommy picked up the metal-based table, smashing it into my head. I felt blood running down my face, but I wasn't beaten yet, even if I looked the part. The table was heavy and, I surmised, had potentially taken a lot of Tommy's energy. He stood in front of me, breathing heavily, fists clenched, waiting to see if his attack had ended the fight.

It should have, but it hadn't. I launched at him, shooting a double leg takedown, sending us both to the beer-sticky floor. This time I wanted to cause as much damage as I could, knowing that I would be held by Odd Job again. Gaining the mounted position, my elbow smashed into his skull. I sensed Odd Job approaching to pull me off his now-bloody boss, so turned and threw a punch that grazed him. He backed away.

In a surreal moment, we all three breathing heavily and carrying the wounds of our battle, said nothing. Then, Tommy suddenly lurched forward, his thumb digging into my eye socket as he barked, "I'm going to fucking kill you now, and no one knows where you are!"

He shouted for his right-hand man to get a knife. It is fair to say that, at this point, I was absolutely frozen by the harsh reality that I had fucked-up big style. Anyone that has ever been in this situation or something similar and tells you they weren't afraid, is either a liar or didn't live to tell the tale.

I had no doubt that he meant it. I knew of his reputation and what he was capable of which, looking back, makes me question why I went to his place looking for a fight. I had one chance. His thumb was digging into my eye, but not enough that I couldn't think. I lifted my knee to my chest and, with a powerful kick, sent him rolling back. The door was only latched, and I pulled it open and made it outside.

At least, I figured, if I was outside and these two small town gangsters were to follow me, then there would be a witness or two, even on a Sunday morning. But nobody followed.

I staggered to my car and drove home at speed. It wasn't over. I knew that I had to finish it, or I would always be looking over my shoulder, fearing for my family's life. Given that they knew where I lived, I decided that I would return that night. I had no choice.

At opening time, I walked up to the door. There, standing like a sentry guarding the Royal household, was Odd Job.

"Tarzan," he said, a smile flashing across his face.

"I want Tommy," I said.

"It's over, Tarzan," he said again, liking his new name for me.

"It's fucking over when I say, and when you lot stop with the fucking Mafia routine," I replied. At that, Tommy appeared in the doorway.

"Tommy let's finish this now, 'round the corner. But this time, just you and me." My mate Gaz stood behind me, eyeing up Odd Job, as if to say, "Let's dance."

Surprisingly, Tommy offered his hand. Now, I have learned through my years of self-defence training that shaking a hand after a fight is like pulling the pin on a live grenade and not expecting it to go off. Something told me this was different.

"Look Gary, you had the balls to face me. We had a fight. It's finished," said Tommy. "I talked to some people and they tell me that the things I have heard that you have said didn't come from you, and that you have only had problems with the lads when they have riled you," he continued.

"Don't drive past my house again, and we are good," I said.

I shook his hand, turned, and walked away.

Rumours started that we had fought over drugs. A ridiculous lie, that made me question the integrity of those that believed it.

19

Tears In Heaven

"No matter how bad your heart is broken, the world doesn't stop for your grief." Faraaz Kazi

We all have situations in our life that can send us off the rails (I seemed to have had my fair share). Sometimes those situations are within our control and sometimes not.

My son, Josh, was happy and healthy when Donna and I found out that we were going to have another baby. In fact, we discovered that we were having twins. A shock to the system, but we knew we would manage and were excited by the news. And that's where life decides to deal you a bad hand; the worst kind. Several months into the pregnancy, after a routine check-up, we were told that there was a problem and that in all likelihood the twins would not go to full term. We sat in a sterile room unable to take in the Dr's words, clinging to a hope that he was wrong and that there had been some kind of mix up. Donna was so distraught that I feared that she would not be able to cope. I was struggling, but I can't imagine what was going through Donna's head. All I know is that she was drowning in despair. I don't think that I have witnessed, to this day, such hopeless all-consuming grief.

Donna had to give birth to the babies, knowing that they wouldn't survive. A position that was so hard for her to be in or accept. Her bravery was astounding and, with a broken heart, she went through the most agonising ordeal that any Mother could imagine being forced into.

The twins were taken to the special baby care unit of the West Cumbria Hospital. We felt the last breath leave their tiny bodies and their grip on life loosen and fail. They were fighters alright, defying the predictions of the medical staff by living for over an hour. And, I must admit, I genuinely thought that they would defy the odds and confound the medical prognosis, but that was not to be.

We were devastated beyond imagination and found it impossible to make sense of the situation. A Priest had come to bless the babies, Shannon and Sarah, and to offer some comfort. Neither Donna nor

I are particularly religious and, I for one, questioned his faith in a God that could do this. Where was his mercy? What was his rationale when murderers, rapists and paedophiles lived full and healthy lives? I didn't just question him, it's more accurate to say that I assaulted him, grabbing him by the neck and shaking him until I collapsed into his arms, tears flowing until my rage subsided.

This wonderful human being took every vile word and insult that came out of my mouth. I apologised, but there really were no words that could take away this pain. We had a funeral and two tiny white coffins carried our babies. Their lives never to be fulfilled, their hopes and dreams stolen before they were even made. We were shattered and broken beyond repair.

Something else died that day. Our relationship, although a little strained, was now crushed against the rocks of this tragedy. There was no lighthouse to guide us through the turbulent waters that lay ahead, no warnings and no hope. We both handled the grief differently. Donna, with dignity, me, self-destructing and crumbling in my own private Hell.

Drink, once again, became a crutch that held me up until I was unable to stand anymore. I woke each morning with the realisation that it was not a sleep-induced nightmare but a sort of Groundhog Day existence that I was cursed to live in. Depression enveloped me. My daylight hours were as black as the coldest night. Any chink of daylight was washed black or grey and the moods reflected this.

What doesn't kill us makes us stronger, or so the saying goes. In my case I became a weak man. Unable to function without a drink. Unable to turn the other cheek and unable to come to terms with the loss I felt. It was only a matter of time before oil and water mixed and the explosion that resulted would have a catastrophic impact on my life.

I didn't care if I lived or died. I drank from early in the day to the close of play, anything to numb the pain and get me through another week. I was angry at a God I wasn't even sure existed. I was angry at myself and those around me but, most of all, I was just plain angry. I was like a pressure cooker that was about to explode. And it wasn't long before it happened in glorious technicolour.

20

I Predict a Riot

"A life spent making mistakes is not only more honorable, but more useful than a life spent doing nothing" George Bernard Shaw

My time in this lawless backwater town had seen me fighting most weekends, and with the scale of violence I was involved in there were bound to be some hair-raising situations.

We have all read about that 'one punch kill' scenario. The story in which an altercation has got out of hand and one of the people involved has lashed-out, hitting someone so hard that they have died as a result. It nearly happened to me one Saturday night after finishing at the club, and a few short weeks after the loss of my daughters.

It had been relatively quiet, and by that, I mean there had probably only been a couple of kick-off's and kick-outs. Gaz, me and his brother, Steve, were all in good spirits on our way home, Steve up ahead, polishing off a kebab, whilst me and Gaz sauntered along unaware that it was all about to go off big time.

I heard a gruff voice up ahead, and then saw this large (that's putting it mildly, this bloke was built like a Weeble, square in body, no neck to speak of, and a head like an oversized walnut) gentleman gesticulating at Steve. Even from some distance we could tell he wasn't asking for directions. Walnuthead was with, I presume, his good lady wife. This woman could clear a field of crows from 20 yards, you get the picture, they had obviously met at one of those *date-in-the dark* parties.

As we approached, we could see that this oversized freak was trying to help himself to Steve's food whilst the scarecrow at his side geed her man on (my hero). I had seen enough.

"What's up mate?" I asked, trying to diffuse the situation.

"Fuck off."

Not the most polite or erudite response, but we were trying to reason with a man that made Forrest Gump look like Stephen Hawking.

"Leave the lad's food, that's not very nice," I reasoned.

"Fuck off." Again, I was surprised by this apes' command of the English language.

"Sorry?" I said, the anger starting to bubble like a volcano about to erupt.

Walnuthead moved towards me.

"Fu…" BANG.

I hit him flush on the jaw, the rest of the expletive never to leave his now-bloody mouth.

His legs collapsed from under his square frame and he slumped to the floor. Scarecrow screamed, but I had no sympathy for her as I was too busy finishing the monster off. I sat astride him punching his now-bouncing skull time and again. I had totally lost it and was out of control. I didn't see a fat Walnut-headed bully, I saw the twins lying in my arms, their fate sealed. The punches weren't aimed at Walnuthead, they were aimed at the force that had decided to take those innocent lives.

The rage was unlike anything I had ever felt. It had little to do with teaching a bully a lesson. Had that been my aim, I would have stopped at the first punch that took him down. No, I wanted to hurt this man. A stranger that had wandered into the wrong area and crossed the wrong person. He was just unlucky.

After what seemed like hours but was in fact seconds, Gaz pulled me off the now prone Walnut-headed lump. I was having none of it, and aimed a kick into his rib cage, or as close as the tyre of fat around his waist would allow. With a start, I came to my senses. Walnuthead lay flat. His face crimson with the blood.

I looked at my hands. There was blood from the knuckles of both hands all the way up my arms and splattered on my face. I looked like I had just ripped the guts from a fresh carcass and blooded myself, much like the aristocracy do on a hunt to celebrate their first kill.

"Go!" shouted Gaz.

I wanted to run but somehow my brain wasn't communicating with my legs.

"You've killed him!" shouted Scarecrow, in-between her earth-shattering screams.

I looked at the grey, lifeless mess that stretched out before me. At last my legs picked up the scrambled signal from my brain and I bolted. I ran until my lungs burned and my heart beat a rhythm I didn't recognise, but one Keith Moon (60's manic drummer whom, it is said, *Animal* from The Muppets was based on) would have been proud of.

Gaz and Steve, who had also taken flight, stopped beside a dark alley and beckoned me over.

"Shit, shit, shit! What the fuck just happened?"

"I think he's dead, Gaz," offered Steve.

I kind of wished I had let the fat bully eat his kebab now, and his observation wasn't what I wanted, or needed, to hear. Sirens punctured the silence, Police, ambulance, perhaps both.

"Right, you two go that way, they'll be looking for three blokes," I said.

I could have curled up and cried. Not for the man lying prone on a hot summer pavement, or for his panicking Mrs. No, selfishly, all I was worried about was myself, my family and the two innocent lads beside me. Mostly, though, I mourned my sense of fair play.

I followed the backstreets home after we split up. I stood outside for a while, waiting, listening, and hoping, eventually going inside. I showered the blood off my hands, arms and face and paced the floor. That night was the longest of my life. I went through every outcome, the Police arriving, the cell door shutting, the jury finding me guilty of manslaughter. I prayed to a God I had long since lost contact with, knowing that it was a waste of time and energy. I knew that I had crossed the line of human decency. I didn't recognise the animal I had become. This man was a victim of all the shit I had been through. He had paid the price for the deaths of Shannon and Sarah. In true denial, I then actually started to believe that I had redressed the balance by hammering this scumbag. He probably had beaten up many an innocent himself, egged on by his vile wife. Maybe I had done society a favour?

My emotions raced and changed time and again until the birdsong and shaft of light through the curtains heralded the start of a new day. Another long day. I called my best mate, Frank. He listened, as he always did and then offered his advice.

"Gary, if this bloke had died it would have been on the news."

It's what I wanted to hear, and I knew he was right. I had some contacts in the area that, like any small-town inhabitants, knew everyone and everyone's business. My relief almost burst from my chest when I heard that the one I called Walnuthead, a known fighter and renowned trouble maker, was ok.

I would like, at this point, to tell you that the fight with Walnuthead had shocked me enough to change my ways, but it didn't. The pain and loss overrode any sense of guilt I might have had and within a month it happened again.

This time, it was an old nemesis that got the brunt of my anger; the Irish Traveller (the Flatley Brother) that had jumped me outside a club a few years back.

Fate has a way of throwing us opportunities to right wrongs and take payback. This was one of those situations. We ended up squaring off in a carpark, again, of all places and, this time, lessons had been learned and we were on our own having, what is known amongst the travelling community as, 'a fair go'. Which *usually* means a bare-knuckle boxing match. Except this time there were no referees or onlookers to call foul play and, as far as I was concerned, this fucker didn't deserve a 'fair go'.

After an initial feeling out process, I launched into a 'blitz attack' which, briefly explained, was me rushing forward throwing left and rights into his thick head. Although he reeled back, and obviously felt each connection, he just smiled at me after the onslaught. This had just one effect. It infuriated me.

I fended off his blows quite easily and caught him with a *pearler*, right on the button. A punch so hard it should have put him on his arse, dreaming of a new caravan and maybe a pony to go with it. But, surprisingly, although he went down, cracking his head on the tarmac, he bounced back up like a demented Jack in the Box. *Jeez, this is harder than it should be*, I thought.

It was only when we danced under the yellow glow of an overhead streetlamp that I realised why he was impervious to the punches. His eyes were wild. Round like saucers. This man was tripping like he had imbibed a bag full of *Dexy's* (Mod slang for amphetamines). I knew then that I could hit this fella with a scud missile and he would keep coming forward. If ever a change of strategy was needed, it was now.

I grinned at his now-bruised and bloody face. The pummelling had done nothing for his looks, he was still an ugly fucker. He was probably fed by catapult as a baby. I don't think he had been educated at a Swiss finishing school either, especially when he spat, "Come on ya' fuckin' cunt! Let's have it!"

My knuckles were sore from trying to rearrange his face anyway, so I was all for taking things to another level - fuck fair play. Where had fair play been when he had set me up for an ambush by his equally-delinquent mate, when they had taken it in turns to jump on my face, ruining my clothes into the bargain?

I threw a jab to his chin, causing him to straighten and stiffen. Seeing the opening, I shot-in for a double leg, lifting him high, before introducing him to the cold, hard concrete that had acted as our battlefield. I felt his skeleton rattle inside as he slammed onto his back.

Not waiting for him to jump up again, I was on top and ready to finish him right there on the cold ground. He turned, trying to get to his knees. I knew he would, and that's all the opportunity I needed to finish him. My right arm snaked around his neck. I locked it onto my left bicep and threw my legs around his waist. There was only the fun part left to do now - The Big Squeeze.

I felt his body go limp as he slumped, the blood cut-off from his brain. That should have been the end of it and, had I been sane, it would have been, but, as we have now established, I wasn't. Far from it, in fact.

I turned him over and, like an artist working on a piece of fresh clay, I went to work. My elbows were the perfect weapon now, given my hands were swollen and probably broken. I wanted this Dickhead to wake up so battered his relatives wouldn't recognise him. This time my mate Gaz wasn't there to stop me, but something else did. A voice inside that said, "Enough."

You could call it common sense, but the beating I had given this poor unfortunate had quenched my thirst for revenge. It wasn't the Traveller I was mad at. It wasn't even the Traveller I was fighting, it was myself. I hadn't dealt with the anger, the helplessness and the grief that was coursing through my veins.

I left my fallen foe lying in a pool of blood, groaning and slowly coming-to. His face was so grotesquely swollen that my new Irish friend resembled Sloth from the Goonies movie ("Hey, you guys!"). I think, from the look of him, I also invented the later, trendy trout pout, as sported by every delusional and desperate millennial starlet frightened by the ravages of time and unable to grow old gracefully. The next day I went back to the carpark, not to see if he was still there, but more to search for my lost watch. I found neither.

My time as DJ/doorman at the club was over, but not before I had caught up with the boss's prodigal son, whom I suspected had started the shit-stirring that had led to the fight with Tommy. I gave him and a couple of his mates a pasting one night and that, for me, was Game, Set, and Match.

Prodigal's brother, a good Thai Boxer that I had swapped some techniques with in the past, came up to me the next night in the pub. The village idiots had gathered, wanting to see me and the brother get into a fight. To be honest, I expected it too. Again, a hand was offered, but this time I didn't question it as a threat.

"Listen mate, that is my brother that you did in. I just wanted to shake your hand, the little fucker has had that coming for a while." We shared a pint, much to the obvious disappointment of the baying mob, and I walked out of the bar.

I realised upon stopping working at the bar that I had become addicted to the fighting. It had become a drug that I craved every Sunday night. I woke up most Mondays covered in bruises and with lumps all over my head, (usually the back where the cowards had waded-in mob handed) and unable to close my hands from the beatings that they had doled out.

My relationship with Josh's Mum had deteriorated. She was sick of the violence and changing behaviour that goes hand in hand with any addiction. We separated, and I moved away from the town, leaving behind the constant threat of repercussion. There would always be someone new to step up, to relight the fire. I had learned that trying to beat an entire town was pointless. This point was proven to me in glorious technicolour one night when, upon leaving a nightclub, I saw a baying mob.

On closer inspection, I saw that what the crowd were watching so intently was a man punching a woman in the face, whilst squeezing her throat. I pushed through the crowd and grabbed the coward by his neck. As he turned around, I punched him, sending his snivelling carcass to the ground. I reached out to the girl to tell her not to worry and was surprised by her spitting in my face and then shouting, "Get off my husband, you bastard!"

I was even more taken aback when the audience of this vile spectacle started swearing at me and pushing me away for intervening.

"Don't get involved, it's between husband and wife."

I couldn't believe it. This was a crowd made up of young and old, men and women, each glaring at me with hatred as if I were the monster.

"Get on with it!" I shouted, pushing my way out of this madness.

If this was the norm in this town, I needed to get out. I felt like Wyatt Earp but, unlike him, I hadn't tamed the Wild West, merely sent a couple of the locals to my own version of Boot Hill (via my boot in their faces).

Despite all this violence and madness, my Jiu-Jitsu training was going well. I was now totally absorbed with BJJ (well, the stuff I had learned from the Gracie Jiu-Jitsu tapes) and had pretty much stopped practicing the Trad Jujitsu that I now held a Black Belt in.

21

One Step Beyond

"Man cannot discover new oceans unless he has the courage to lose sight of the shore." Andre Gide

It was around 1997-98 that the first Brazilian Jiu-Jitsu Black Belt moved to the UK. A gentleman by the name Chen Moraes.

A buzz went around the UK Martial Arts community like wildfire. I *had* to get involved. Unfortunately, for me, Chen set up his school in London. I lived in Cumbria, but it might as well have been Rio de Janiero. It is worth mentioning that a Blue Belt in BJJ was as *rare as rocking horse shit* in the UK around this time. Those that held the then-coveted Blue Belt had travelled across the pond to America to train with the Gracie family. To me and those like me, a Blue Belt was *God in a Gi*. Hard to believe in these days of plenty.

Chen had set up the UK BJJ Association and was soon advertising competitions. I was elated at the prospect of testing my video-gleaned knowledge against a real live BJJ opponent. So, with a new goal in mind, I trained like a man possessed. My morning 5-mile run was interspersed with sprint training. I continued to lift weights, train my Judo and did as much drilling and rolling as possible, usually twice a day, every day.

The first competition was in London and was a British Open tournament. I signed up without hesitation. My Gi now proudly sported the UK BJJ badge that Chen had sent me upon registration, and I felt ready to go. My academy hired a bus and off we went. There were two of us competing, but the bus was full of students and friends excited at the prospect of watching their first BJJ tournament. We set off for London before the sun had even chosen a hat to put on.

It was going to be a long day as we were setting off back home after the last bout of the day. Upon reaching the Capital city, my initial excitement turned to apprehension. Here I was, about to compete in the biggest tournament I had ever entered, watched by my legion of students, all thinking I was untouchable. It's called the big fish in a small pond effect. But I felt like I was entering a huge ocean as a minnow and, worse, as the main course for the waiting sharks to devour.

London was so far removed from the small town where I taught Jiu-Jitsu. The hustle and bustle made me tired even from my window seat of the coach. Finally, we pulled up at the sports centre, an impressive building in the heart of the capital's opulent Kensington. This place reeked of money. We must have looked like a bunch of hillbillies to these sophisticated Southerners, all "Ey up," and dodgy haircuts. But it didn't matter, we weren't there to walk the catwalk. Our goal, or rather my goal, was to compete and test myself.

The tournament was well attended, with around 200 competitors all warming-up, ready to throw down and enter the realms of competitive BJJ. The first thing I noticed, just from observing the warm-up, was how supple some of these people were. I had never been able to achieve the splits, save for one time when I slipped on some ice outside my house, left leg was heading due South whilst right leg decided to explore the North. Either way, it was bloody painful and affected my voice upon recovery. My warm-up was a little more traditional. Press-ups, sit-ups and a sort of Karate-type stretch that I never really felt any benefit from doing but had always done it anyway.

I noticed that there was some activity around the desks that were set up. A group of students, all wearing the Chen Moraes Anaconda BJJ Gi, were checking out the brackets. I decided to have a nosey and see when I was up. I kind of wished I hadn't looked. We all know the story of the fighter being beaten before they step on the mat, well, this is mine.

The name next to mine was familiar. Not just familiar, more a household name in British Martial Arts. Take a bow, the great Rick Young. Rick was the original ambassador of the cross-training fraternity. He had travelled to America to train under the Gracie's before anyone had even heard the name, and a while before UFC1. Rick was a skilled Judoka Black Belt into the bargain and a consummate professional Martial Artist. This was it, a seven-hour bus trip to London to be wiped out in my first fight.

After a while I started to get excited about the bout. I might pull off an upset and beat this man. A man who, up until that day, I had only ever seen on the front cover of my favourite Martial Arts magazines. He looked different without the staples going through his middle.

The time had come. My name was called first, the silence from the crowd deafening. In contrast, when Rick was called to the Tatami, the arena went into a frenzy. To say that I felt like a lamb to the slaughter is an understatement. You could feel the excitement from the spectators. The chant of Rick's name grew louder as the man himself stood before me. It's at this stage that I wished I had just walked over and shook his hand but, no, ever the showman, I had to make the sign of a cross (think Catholic priest).

If ever a wrong signal was given, then this was it. Rick didn't seem to mind my attempt at humour, and why should he, I might as well have taken the announcer's mic and declared, "I am beaten." At least it made my friends laugh. After the handshake and fist-bump we were ready to go.

I knew Rick was a good judo player so, rather than wait to be launched through the air, I took the initiative and attacked first. My grips were good, and I felt strong as I pushed my right foot onto Rick's hip and pulled guard, hoping for an arm bar on the way. Rick sensed it, and we both started to jockey for the best position. I locked my legs around his waist making him work to try and pass my guard, occasionally reaching into his collar for the cross choke. It seemed like an age before Rick opened my guard and took side control. I fought to regain position, but his pressure was immense, and I felt the best course of action was to relax before exploding again in an attempt to get to my knees.

Rick was working for a Kimura. And, although he had a good grip, I fought it off, spinning my hips to regain guard. I managed half guard before the wily Scot passed again, this time to North South. He still wanted the Kimura and I knew it. I grabbed my belt hoping to thwart his advance. Rick maintained position but then, in a move I had never seen or felt before, he used my Gi to trap my arm to my belt. He wound the cloth underneath, affording him the leverage to prize my hand free. With this, he secured the Kimura and, using his position, rolled me to my side and cranked the arm into position to finish the submission. I resisted for as long as I could, but my arm reached an angle that, by the sound of the clicking, was not healthy. I stood, dejected but proud, as I saw that I had lasted almost to the end of the allotted time of the bout.

Rick politely shook my hand and left the mat. I watched the rest of the tournament from the sidelines with a cold compress on my now-stiffening shoulder. Rick went on to annihilate the rest of the people in the category and make it to the winner's podium. At the end of the matches I was surprised to see him walking across the mat in my direction. He offered his hand and, in his rich Edinburgh accent said, "I really enjoyed our bout. You are very strong and have potential."

You could have knocked me down with a feather as he continued, "If you are ever in Edinburgh, come and train with me. No charge."

I might have lost the fight, but I felt like the champion that day. Rick Young probably can't even recall me or our bout, but his actions and words of encouragement meant so much to me.

I certainly have never forgotten it, and never will.

22

As Thick as Thieves

"Revenge is sweet and not fattening." Alfred Hitchcock

Although I had found an outlet for my aggression and I wasn't going out looking for fights, one night I was to revert to my old ways. I didn't set out looking to fight that night but something in me snapped and a name from the past was the catalyst.

It had been many years since my family had been robbed of the meagre possessions and Christmas presents, we had in our less than salubrious place of residence; a caravan, set in a field in the middle of nowhere. That awful Christmas was hanging around my mind like a bad smell. Ever since I had heard the name and description of the man responsible, I had wanted to take revenge. The Police hadn't been able to prove anything or arrest anyone, but the crime fitted this scumbag's usual modus operandi. His calling card, if you will, was not only to take anything that wasn't nailed down, but also to defecate all over the scene and trash the place. He certainly did that to our place.

He was a particularly nasty piece of work who, according to the Police, would not have hesitated to assault anyone that had tried to stop him. He didn't care if you were young, old, infirm or whatever, he used violence as a knee-jerk reaction and didn't seem to possess a conscience. Not content with just a push or a slap, this bastard would seriously maim if he needed to escape the scene. Prison was an occupational hazard that came with the job description, thieving twat.

It was only by chance that I caught up with him one night many summers later. I was having a Sunday evening beverage with my mate Gaz. The bar was a real drinker's pub, not like the soulless bars that we have today. It was all spit, sawdust and real ale. Around the small bar area stood a group of older men, hardened drinkers all. They must have been in their late-thirties to early-forties which, to me at the time, seemed old. Their conversation matched their dress sense, loud and not particularly clean. There was much boasting and merriment. Nothing wrong in that, we were in a pub and not a library. Something about the blonde-haired and much-bearded bloke, who seemed to be the *main man*, caught my attention. He was quiet, listening as his cronies vied for his attention.

Occasionally, he would laugh or chip in a word or two but, overall, he was silent, as if looking at the scene from afar. I then heard someone address him by name, causing the hairs on the back of my neck to stand to attention and set my heart beating faster. The name was the same Christian name of the faceless invader of my childhood home. Nothing strange in that if this bloke had a common name like John, Dave or Gary, for that matter, but he didn't. In fact, in all my years, I had never known anyone with this name. It was, I think, of Polish or even Russian descent.

Anyway, I knew it was the same man that had caused the pain to my family. I just knew it. This was a small town, the chances of another man of his age having that name were too small. But I needed to be sure. I got up from my table, leaving Gaz looking a bit confused, and walked up to the group. I tapped the man I suspected on the shoulder and when he turned, I said, "Is your name Ima Thieving Bastard?" (for legal reasons I can't give the real name).

"Yes," came the reply. "Who wants to know?"

I looked at him for longer than was probably comfortable for both of us before saying, "Gary Savage. You don't know me, just like you don't know many of the people you have robbed in your life."

He turned his head to look at his mates and that's all I needed.

Bang. A sweet right cross found its mark. He crumpled forward, and I hit him with three or four rapid shots before he went down. And that is when it really got interesting. His mates, as if one, dived on me. Some holding me, some trying to punch me. We all ended up on the floor, Thieving Bastard underneath a scrum that was flailing wildly. I was on top of the bastard, my hand went to his throat and I squeezed. I could feel him gasping for air. It felt good, but it would have felt a bit better had I not had half a ton of pissed dickheads on top of me, punching and grabbing at me at the same time. I was hauled off eventually, given a few punches whilst held, and then I was thrown out of the door, landing flat on my face.

Seconds later I was joined by Gaz who had also been politely shown the door. I could hear the group inside shouting and could tell that they were panicking about their now stretched-out and prone leader. That's when I went in again. I rushed through the door knocking the stooping clowns aside like tenpins. Before they regained their feet, I was on top of Mr Thieving Bastard again, pummelling his head for all I was worth. The kicking I took from the group was worth it and, eventually, I was again thrown out onto the pavement. This time the sound of bolt securing door was the only sound from inside.

I was done. I didn't care about the mob, I had got my revenge and given the bastard something to think about. He had been visited by the Ghost of Christmas Past and, hopefully, he understood the hurt he had caused all those years ago.

Thieving Bastard wasn't the only light-fingered dimwit I had a run-in with during this time. On this occasion, however, I was to be surprised by the reaction of the Thin Blue Line.

I was at a friend's house one evening after enjoying a night in a local pub. There were four of us at the house, my mate, his new lady friend, me, and my then partner. The night was full of laughter and daftness and the atmosphere was buzzing. That is until a loud banging on the door startled us all and brought us back to reality. Mark, my mate, went to the window and, after peering through a crack in the curtains, exclaimed to his girlfriend, "It's your dickhead ex."

The banging got worse. I thought the door was going to come off the hinges when Sue (Mark's girlfriend) got up and went to the door. I could hear muffled voices and then the living room door opened and in stepped The Ex. He had the look of a half-starved interbreed. Tall, not particularly handsome or, for that matter, ugly. His most remarkable feature, if it could be called that, was the number of dodgy tattoos that adorned his scrawny frame, from neck to hands.

"What the fuck is this?" he said. Obviously not the most observant of chaps.

After a second or two of the interbreed banging on, his ex-girlfriend screaming, and Mark trying to placate the moron, I had heard enough.

"Why don't you just go home and sleep off whatever it is that you have taken?"

Interbreed didn't like this and started towards me. I couldn't react as my girlfriend was sitting on my knee. He grabbed for an ornate model cottage that adorned the mantelpiece and without even a by your leave, smashed it into my head.

Adrenalin, or just plain anger, blocked out any pain. I pushed my girlfriend off me, aware that blood was pouring from the wound inflicted by the model but still in charge of my reactions and, fuelled by rage, I flew at the tattooed prick. He raised the cottage again. This time I moved and, with a hefty right hand, sent the moron reeling backwards. As if attached by an invisible chord, I followed, throwing rights and lefts until he sprawled onto the sofa.

He covered up, screaming for me to stop, but I pulled him to his feet. He made a pathetic attempt to use the ornament again. I locked his arm and applied a figure-four lock, making him drop the makeshift weapon. Now, it was the fun part. I turned his arm until a loud crack signalled a break or at least a good dislocation. Either way, the party wasn't over yet. He screamed in agony as I threw him back on the sofa, his face bloody, his arm dangling at his side.

Target was locked on. Bang. I hit his jaw with a hard Muay Thai shin kick, sending him straight to the land of nod. It was only then that I heard the screaming and crying from the other people in the house. It became apparent that they had never witnessed this level of violence. The problem was, I hadn't finished the job. I still had to take out the trash. I grabbed Sleeping Beauty by the scruff of his neck, dragging the limp body through the house until I came to the still open door. One last kick put the scumbag out.

The following day, a familiar knock signalled the arrival of the *Boys in Blue*. I was politely asked to accompany them to the Police station to 'answer a few questions'. *Here we go again*, I thought, but how wrong I was to be on this occasion.

Led through the station, I was amazed to be treated so well by the officers that had picked me up. They acted positively human towards me.

"What's this about?" I tried to bluff my way out of the impeding arrest.

"Gary, look. We know it was you that gave #### a good kicking last night."

Right, I thought, *do I go down the no-comment route early, or wait for the duty solicitor?*

"Gary, do you know who this lad is?" continued the officer.

"Erm, no. It was self-defence - look at my head."

I had decided to get my side of the story in before they did the whole good cop/bad cop routine. But something was not quite stacking up. There was no bad cop. They were really being decent with me, even offering tea and biscuits.

"Listen Gary. That lad you messed up is a complete twat."

Go on.

"He robbed an elderly lady at knife point a while ago," said Cop #1.

"She was too terrified to press charges," added Cop #2. "He had a balaclava on, but the stupid prick has a distinctive tattoo on his right hand, the hand with which he held the knife under the Old Dears' throat. She described it in detail, even the bit that had his equally dense brother's name on," he continued.

This wasn't going too bad.

"We have to be seen to bring you in," said Cop #1.

"We have been hoping to nick that vermin for a while," continued Cop #2.

"You giving the dick the beating of his life maybe hasn't gone down too badly with us," smiled Cop #1.

Anyway, the upshot was that I was released without charge. I got thanked for giving the scum a good hiding. My roommate, Frank (no stranger to the cells himself), thought I was joking when I relayed the story upon my return. The Police might not have had much time for me but, when it came to a piece of low life vermin that robbed old dears at knife point, I was a saint.

23

Changing Man

"Your past is not your destiny. You can change your future at any moment." Anthon St. Maarten

I was done with fighting.

At least on the tarmac. My focus now was on my competitive martial arts journey. I had righted some wrongs, dealt out some of my own brand of justice to people that, in my world view, deserved everything they got. But there comes a time when you must take a decision to stay away from certain situations and people that can reignite the flame and throw you straight back into the fire. The more you are trained to fight, the less you want to get involved in mindless acts of violence.

It was as if you had two shadows. The second one being the constant threat of reprisal that keeps you looking over your shoulder. Nothing good ever comes from carrying a reputation as a 'fighter'. I don't mean in the sporting context, I'm talking about the brutality of chaotic violence, where there are no rules, no referees and little in the way of conscience if someone gets hurt.

I had a conscience. I *didn't want* the constant battle between the good and the bad. The good being when you have stood up and tried to do the right thing, and the bad being the pain you have caused, whether the person deserved it or not. I was, and am, intrinsically a very fair and good person. I believe that we can get pulled into situations as a result of the choices we make, and I had certainly made some bad calls in my past.

Walking away from trouble is very difficult if you tread the path of violence. You beat yourself up worse than any opponent if you have stepped back and walked away from a fight. You know in your heart that most 'street fighters' can't actually fight. And you know that, as a trained fighter, you could destroy the person in your crosshairs with ease. You also know that you would, more than likely, destroy your own future.

I have had, in later years, to take the decision to refrain from taking violent action against people that were in the wrong, getting in my face, and causing trouble. It is hard, but it would be harder throwing away my future career or losing my liberty for a trivial matter. Ego is a great matchmaker in street fighting circles. People are always trying to prove something. Either to themselves or others.

Martial Arts are all about losing the Ego. If you can do this, then you can become free and live a peaceful life. Martial Artists don't train to fight in the street. They train so that they don't have to fight in the street. There is a saying, "It is better to be a warrior in a garden than a gardener in a war."

From here on in I intended to enjoy the garden and avoid unnecessary wars.

24

London Calling

"If things go wrong, don't go with them." Roger Babson

After my, somewhat disappointing, debut in London, I was back in our glorious Capital city again in 1999 to try and redeem myself.

It was the *Big One* as far as British BJJ was concerned. This was Chen's European BJJ Championships. I had taken some lessons from my defeat at the hands of the great Rick Young. I knew my strengths, but also my weaknesses. I incorporated some Boxing and Thai Boxing for stamina. I ate healthily and wasn't drinking. My students became my sparring partners, pushing me hard in each roll. I was focused and determined that this was my time. Anything but a place on the podium would be a disappointment.

The drive to London found me in a pensive mood. I was as ready as I could be. I was prepared. I knew what to expect. The first disappointment was that I had no one in my weight category. Automatic Gold. But that was not why I had travelled for 5 hours. I was put into the weight category above and into an age category below mine. No worries, I came to fight.

My first opponent felt very heavy. We gripped; I pulled guard by pulling my foot in his hip and falling back. As soon as I landed, I spun the arm bar. It was as tight as Chuck Norris's Stretch Wranglers. My opponent gave a scream and tapped-out. My first submission win in a BJJ competition.

The elation was immense. I always believed in being a gentleman, so reached down and held out my hand to help my fallen foe back to his feet. As I walked off the tatami (mats), a man I instantly recognised came over and shook my hand. Carl Fisher, AKA the Fighting Photographer, was a journalist with the top Martial Arts magazines. A true gent and, as a Northerner, I felt an instant camaraderie amongst all these Southerners.

Carl was very supportive, offering advice from the mat side. My next fight went the same way; same move, same outcome. And then it got interesting. The Final. I had watched my opponent absolutely dominate his two previous opponents. He was skilled, using techniques I wasn't familiar with to control and submit his way to the final. I came out hard.

Andy Farrell was a behemoth. Muscles on muscles. There was no way I was rolling over, though. We gripped, and he literally pulled me off my feet. I felt like I was on the fairground whizzer. I hit the ground hard. My first instinct was *hands in collar and squeeze until he went to sleep*. He didn't play ball. My guard was considered hard to pass, at least it was by everyone else that I rolled with. This guy cut through me like a hot knife through butter.

Having passed, he went to knee on belly. Up until that point in my Jiu-Jitsu career I had never experienced what I later came to appreciate as 'pressure'. I felt the air being sucked out of my body. His knee drove so far into me I thought of calling the Police to say that I had been violated. This man was on another level. I never tapped-out. For the second time in my brief BJJ career the ref threw in the towel. Upon protestation he claimed I had turned blue. Regardless, I came home with a Silver medal, and I had made two new friends in Carl Fisher and Andy Farrell.

My next move after my first taste of a BJJ medal, was to try and change my training up. I knew I was basically a small fish in a big pond. I was frustrated, there were no BJJ Blue Belts in the area and the nearest Black Belt was in London.

25

Little By Little

"Do not go where the path may lead, go instead where there is no path and leave a trail." Ralph Waldo Emerson

So, here I was, like many other UK Martial Artists, desperate to find someone that could teach me authentic BJJ.

In the early days, when we had first seen the UFC tapes, there was a wave of interest in Gracie Jiu-Jitsu and, much like the effect that Bruce Lee had in the 70's when Chinese immigrants suddenly remembered that they were Kung Fu experts, it seemed that every jujitsu school started to place a greater emphasis on the ground game.

Soon, these traditional Japanese Jujitsu schools were adding the caveat to their advertising 'Brazilian *style* Jiu-Jitsu'. The word 'style' was their saving grace, as they weren't teaching Gracie Jiu-Jitsu at all. It was a clever marketing ploy that they knew wouldn't hold water for long, but it would, as it was designed to do, bring in some naive people that wouldn't know the difference between traditional *jits* and the Gracie Jiu-Jitsu that they wanted to learn.

Enrolment at these trad jujitsu schools flourished, but it was only a matter of time before cracks started to appear and the disillusioned spread their net wider in search of the 'real' BJJ that had caught their imagination. Chen Moraes, the mastermind behind the UK's first BJJ competitions, was the first Brazilian, as far as my recollection goes, to touchdown on UK soil. And, although his influence cannot be ignored, he was soon followed and quickly usurped by arguably the greatest of all the early UK BJJ pioneers, Mauricio Motta Gomes.

If Chen had got the planning permission, then Motta Gomes was the man that laid the foundations upon which the UK BJJ scene was built. He truly was the Founding Father. Mauricio Motta Gomes was no ordinary BJJ Black Belt (if such an animal existed), he was one of the few BJJ Black Belts to be graded by the legendary Rolls Gracie, arguably the best of the Gracie family. Rolls' life had been cut short following a hang-gliding accident and, at the time of his death, he had only awarded 10 Black Belts. Mauricio first set up shop in Birmingham, where he taught out of an old custard factory. Later, he moved to London and taught in a few locations across the city.

BJJ's pace in the UK was starting to gain some momentum, albeit slow, but at least it was moving in the right direction.

Although the UK BJJ rolling stone was starting to gather some moss in the South of England, it was a different story in the North.

The North had some Blue Belts that had started to share their knowledge, but it would still be some time before we had a Black Belt north of the Watford gap. Northerners are resilient, and besides, we are used to the South getting the lion's share of great opportunities. In short, we weren't discouraged, and armed with the few BJJ moves we knew (or thought we knew), we tried to keep the flame burning.

Looking back now, it was comical. I, like many of the early BJJ junkies, wore the BJJ kimono, but still tied around my waist was my Japanese Black Belt. We, or certainly I, wasn't one of the Japanese Jujitsu instructors cashing in, I just liked the BJJ Gi's, and, more importantly, we knew no better. Back in the day, there really wasn't much choice of Gi. It was mainly *Krugen*, a heavily-badged gi that epitomized the fighting spirit of the art.

If you liked the Vale Tudo aspect, you would sport a pair of *budgie smugglers* with the 'Bad Boy' insignia, resplendent with a pair of fierce looking fangs emblazoned across the butt cheeks (not a good look really). Harbinger were the MMA glove of choice, mainly because, like the Gi and the shorts, there just wasn't other brands as readily available. Even if we knew very little, at least we had all the gear (all the gear, no idea).

Around this time a book appeared that, to me at least, offered some new grappling moves and was my go-to for teaching for at least a couple of years. The book, 'The Fighter's Notebook', was a huge piece of work. It retailed at a ridiculous price, and really was poor quality, black and white pictures with limited explanation. It was basically a file that the authors had rushed out in order to corner a growing and exciting new market. Having said that, I had no hesitation in shelling out the money. And, although it was a *no Gi* instructional, it was packed with great technique and so it became my class curriculum for a good few years so, I got my money's worth.

26

Welcome to the Jungle

"A good traveler has no fixed plans and is not intent on arriving."
Lao Tzu

The first time I trained with a member of Brazilian Jiu-Jitsu's *First Family* was around 1998 when Carley Gracie came over to teach a seminar in the West Midlands.

Carley was the 11th child of Grand Master Carlos Gracie and is widely regarded as the founding father of Brazilian Jiu-Jitsu in the United States, having relocated from his native Brazil in 1972. His moniker, 'The Lion', perfectly described his aggressive yet technical style which ultimately saw him winning state and national BJJ titles before he switched to the bloody and brutal Vale Tudo (anything goes) proving ground contests made popular in his home country. Perhaps Carley's greatest triumph came in 1994 when he was caught up in a legal battle with his cousin Rorian. Rorian (the brains behind the UFC concept) had tried to trademark the name Gracie Jiu-Jitsu with the intention of stopping the wider Gracie family from using the name to publicise and promote their art. The legal battle seemed as barbaric as any of the families fights on the mat or the ring, but the ruling went the way of Carley after a jury found that Rorian did not have a valid federal trademark. The landmark victory, along with UFC 1, is believed by many to be the catalyst for Gracie Jiu-Jitsu's vast growth across the USA and subsequently the rest of the world. It was therefore fitting that Carley would be the first Gracie to teach in the United Kingdom after he accepted an invitation from Ross Ianocarro the President of Tai Jutsu Kai.

I was not going to miss the chance of training with a member of this legendary dynasty. Come Hell or high water, I was going to be there. The training hall was rammed with eager students by the time I arrived, all excited, as was I, to see what a real Gracie Jiu-Jitsu black belt could do. I had this man pegged as unbeatable before he had even opened his mouth to address his adoring public.

Carley was a big man and you could tell just from the presence he gave that he didn't suffer fools, although the fact that he kept his ankle white socks on during the seminar made him appear that bit more human. Either that, or he didn't appreciate the typically inclement English weather.

Carley spoke good English and he taught with an ease that only comes from complete mastery of your chosen art. He demonstrated a few techniques that I had seen on the 'Gracie Jiu-Jitsu Basics' VHS. The same ones I must have watched and practiced a thousand times by then. But it was the way he moved and the attention to the smallest detail that set him apart from any Japanese Jujitsu master I had been training with up until this point. I realised to my frustration that I had been doing most of the moves wrong. In short, Carley's Jiu-Jitsu looked like a totally different Jiu-Jitsu, which of course it was. When he showed the scissor sweep it blew my mind. How had I never thought of doing this most simplistic of sweeps when someone was in my guard? I practiced it religiously when I got back home, and the first time I swept someone with it I felt unbeatable (I still use it to this day). My Jiu-Jitsu, I realised, was all about using strength. And, although I had won some BJJ bouts, I now realised that there was little in the way of skill and technique in my application. This was the *wake up and smell the coffee* moment I needed, and it set me on the right road, even if that road was a long and seemingly endless one, towards Jiu-Jitsu enlightenment.

Carley Gracie's visit and subsequent visits to the UK certainly helped to raise the consciousness in all that attended his seminars, even if some die-hard traditionalists scoffed and closed their minds to the possibilities that adding the techniques might benefit them.

The second time I attended a Carley Gracie seminar he, more or less, taught the same techniques. I witnessed a high-ranking and much-respected Japanese Jujitsu Black Belt puff out his breath heavily and walk off the mats saying, "I already learned this move."

For me, it was as if I had been given a glimpse of the *promised land*. My resolve to one day achieve not only a Blue Belt in this great art, but maybe even the coveted Black Belt, absorbed my every thought. Back then, I had only ever seen a handful of Blue Belts as they were as rare as hen's teeth in the United Kingdom. But, as some great Chinese philosopher called Confucius once said, "The journey of a thousand miles starts with a single step."

In 1998 it was more a case of one step forward, three steps back but, even if my progress was slow, at least I was trying. Carley Gracie played a major part in the burning ambition that now consumed my every waking hour. I didn't realise it back then, but I would eventually train and meet other members of the Gracie family, including Royce and Rickson Gracie.

But it was to be Renzo Gracie that made the biggest impression on me.

Renzo Gracie

If Carley Gracie was the Lion of the family, then his nephew, Renzo Gracie, was a different kind of predator.

Renzo is the Grandson of the late Carlos Gracie. He holds a 6th degree black belt in Jiu-Jitsu and teaches out of his New York academy, where he has trained a host of MMA superstars including George St-Pierre, Matt Serra and Frankie Edgar. But Renzo is best known for his 'do or die' approach to fighting.

Renzo famously said, "The lion is the King of the jungle but, put him in the ocean and he becomes just another meal." Renzo Gracie certainly typified the shark. Never one to back down from a challenge. Renzo, perhaps more than any other, epitomises the warrior spirit that is synonymous with the Gracie name.

A year after Carley had visited these shores, Renzo Gracie touched down. If I had been excited about training under Carley, who, if I'm being honest, I had never heard of before his seminar, then Renzo was someone to really get the Jiu-Jitsu juices flowing.

The hall was full by the time I arrived. I had travelled down with my friend, another Japanese Jujitsu Black Belt called John. John wasn't as taken by the whole BJJ bug that had certainly bitten me, but he liked to roll and wanted to add a few techniques to his arsenal. I didn't realise it at the time, but the attendees were the future *Who's Who* of UK BJJ and MMA pioneers. Ian Freeman and Dave Briggs, to name drop two.

Little did I know but this seminar was to play a huge part in the UK's development in terms of Brazilian Jiu-Jitsu. Mauricio Motta Gomes introduced Renzo who, until he spoke, gave off an unnerving presence. He had been sitting alone on a window ledge, staring out at the legion of pasty-faced wannabe Jiu-Jitsu students.

I became paranoid that I was being stared-out. My nerves were certainly playing tricks, causing my stomach to flip a few somersaults.

Renzo gathered us around, and soon his warm personality put us at ease. The man had an infectious laugh and the attendees were soon rolling in the aisles (not literally). His techniques were beautifully executed and explained in such a way as to reach everyone. John and I were busy trying out the arm bar Renzo had demonstrated when my world nearly fell out of my pants.

John, in his broad Coventry accent, shouted across the room, "Rickson (pronouncing the R), have you a minute, mate?"

I could have crawled into a hole right there and then. Talking out of the side of my mouth, as if that was subtle, I said, "It's Renzo, you clown."

John, not batting an eyelid, just waved his hand in the air, as if it were the most natural thing in the world and just in case any one of the 100 or so students had missed his gaffe. Renzo had heard the faux pas but, if offended, he didn't show it.

"Yes, my brother?" he asked John. My face must have been scarlet but, seeing that Renzo was cool with being called Rickson, I awaited his instruction. John performed his take on the arm bar to which Renzo, grinning from ear to ear proclaimed, "That's better than me, my brother."

Damn, now I was wishing I had called him Rickson and got to be complimented for my technique. The jammy git. The techniques were more advanced than I had learned at Carley's sessions. Renzo really wanted us to see authentic BJJ and not the watered-down stuff that we had been exposed to on some of the VHS tapes we were forced to buy if we wanted to learn.

Two hours passed in a heartbeat and after we rolled there was a Q & A session. Everyone wanted to ask Renzo about his fights, and Renzo was happy to oblige, demonstrating his flair as a raconteur. He told of his fight with the Judo Black Belt, Ben Spijkers, who he had beaten soundly and then stomped on him after the stoppage. Renzo explained that, the night before the fight, Spijkers had found out what room he was staying in and had had his entourage ring the room and bang on the door all night. Laughing, he said, "When I beat him, I was still pissed at him, so I decided to stomp on him."

The crowd, not knowing the back-story, had booed him and he was given a warning for unsportsmanlike behaviour. Renzo laughed again and said, "And, I would do the same again to the Motherfucker."

After all the history and the stories had been shared, a voice at the back said, "I have a question."

"Yes, my friend?" replied Renzo.

"I keep getting stuck in side control, can you show me a technique to get out, please?"

Renzo replied, "Of course, my friend, but I will show you against someone bigger than you and me."

Renzo scoured the room before settling on what I would describe as the largest human being I had ever seen. His ears were gnarled into perfect cauliflower patterns, his muscles had muscles and his neck was as thick as an oak tree.

"You, my friend. Do you know the hold down?" Renzo asked Man Mountain.

Jeez, this bloke looked like he was *born* holding some poor unfortunate in side control. Renzo laid down and gestured for the Man Mountain to hold him for all he was worth. My heart was racing. This could end very badly. It looked like water would have a job getting out from under this bloke's vice-like grip.

The whole room went silent and you could have heard a pin drop as Renzo wiggled underneath for what seemed like a very uncomfortable age. The only sound was the occasional laugh from beneath the Man Mountain's death grip. And then, just as I had given up hope and decided to cover my eyes, it happened.

I'm still not sure, to this day, some twenty years later, how or what I witnessed, but happen it did. Man Mountain was launched into the air, before reconnecting with the mat. Renzo's legs had encircled his vast frame and an arm bar was applied. I can't describe the feeling, but it was something magical. John stared open-mouthed along with the rest of those who witnessed this scene. BJJ was wizardry, and this confirmed it.

There was no going back for me now. I knew what I had to do, even if I was a little unsure as to just how I would do it. In some ways, I was elated at the thought of being taught these ninja moves, but a part of me was even more frustrated. We were a long way off having regular access to a Blue Belt, let alone a Black Belt.

Although Mauricio Motta Gomes was in 'Brum' and Chen Moraes in London, these great coaches might just as well have been on the moon. I was earning crap money for working all the hours God sent, and I had a family to support. All I could do was drill the new techniques and wait.

News was reaching us that the USA had become the foster home for hundreds of BJJ Black Belts. You couldn't blame them for choosing the States, they had a great climate, surfing, and it was the home of Hollywood. We, on the other hand, had rain, dark nights and cold mornings. Oh, and we had a nation that was obsessed with watching a bunch of overpaid prats kicking a pig's bladder around a pitch, whilst the so-called fans kicked each other around the terraces. Hardly Hollywood.

The chosen few took training opportunities where we could. I also bought any video and read anything I got my hands on. These days there is a plethora of information out there via the internet and YouTube, but we were still wandering a barren desert with no sign of a watering hole.

27

All or Nothing

"It is only after you've stepped outside your comfort zone that you begin to change, grow and transform." Roy T. Bennett

The year 2000 sees mass panic over-riding common sense. Planes are thought to be at risk of falling out of the skies, and all the computers will crash as the clock strikes twelve on New Year's Day.

Back in the day, competitions were few and far between. MMA: hardly any. BJJ: occasionally, but a new beast was emerging. Something in-between, not MMA and not pyjama-wearing fighting, either.

This new phenom was called Submission Grappling. You could wear the same gear as the latter-day MMA stars, i.e. *budgie smugglers*, a short so tight, even your Mother would question your sexuality. I had gone as far as I could on my own and decided that, if I wanted to achieve my goals in Jiu-Jitsu and MMA, then I had to be prepared to move. I had seen a few good articles in Martial Arts Illustrated magazine about some capable coaches in the Manchester area.

I applied for a place at the University of Central Lancashire and packed all my worldly goods and went in search of education, both academic and to further my Martial aspirations. It was hard, particularly as it meant leaving my two sons, but I figured that I would be a better Father if I got a job that paid well as opposed to a Dad that they visited in jail.

University was a breeze, really. The hours meant that I had lots of time to train. I travelled to Manchester to the Van Dang Martial Arts School and enquired about training under Karl Tanswell as a private student. On the day I was meant to meet Karl, the train was delayed and when I found the gym, Karl had gone. Coupled with this setback, I had the hangover from Hell and really could have done without the hassle of a wasted journey.

One of Karl's assistant coaches, Gavin Boardman, was at the gym and, after a bit of wrangling, he called Karl to explain my situation.

Karl asked Gavin to put me through my paces, a grappling roll, to see what level I was at. Although he was lighter than me, his ground game was good, and we had quite a battle, neither giving quarter. We rolled for well over an hour. No submissions were made but we both knew we had been in a war. Afterwards, we shook hands, a new-found respect between us.

On arriving back home, I was pleased to get a call from Karl saying that Gavin was complimentary about my ground game and he would be willing to take me as a student. My training would start the following Saturday. I was about to become a member of Defence Unlimited (later to morph into Straight Blast Gym (SBG)).

I wasn't to stay at SBG long though, leaving after I was awarded my Blue Belt from Matt Thornton, but I did get some good rolling in with the team, and made a great friend in Gavin Boardman.

28

Roll With It

"He who conquers himself is the mightiest warrior." Confucious

It was during my time at SBG Manchester that I really focused on building my own gym.

I was a competent grappler and could throw a half-decent punch and kick. I found a room in Lancaster Sports Centre and put up posters advertising the start of "Total fight Jiu-Jitsu", later to morph into "The Grappler's Academy". My training day was Saturday, 10.00-12.00pm.

I had a great room that had judo matting and was clean and warm. The only thing I didn't have was a student. That is, until a bald, bespectacled gentleman by the name of Nigel walked through the door. Erudite and polite, he asked if I would teach him. Looks can be deceptive.

Nigel proved, as the weeks went by, that he was a tough little fellow that was quick to learn and eager to progress. It was only Nigel and I for the first few weeks until word started to spread that there was a local place teaching Mixed Martial Arts. Two soon became three and, shortly after, we had moved into double figures. I had an open-door policy, but the training was tough with all-out sparring and pressure-testing of techniques through real combat.

We had every local 'hard man' visit the gym. Usually, they wanted to see if the system was effective and, since my way was to prove it and myself, there were many challenge fights. Not all challenge fights ended badly. One that still makes me smile and led to a friendship that still survives involved a local man called Andy. Upon first impression, Andy didn't look like the atypical tough guy. He was shorter than me (and I am only 5' 8" in heels), slim, to the point of looking half-starved, and not exactly in the first flush of youth but, and this is a big but, that adage, 'don't judge a book by its cover', was about to be proven true. Andy walked into the gym about half-way through a session.

"What's all this about?" was his opening gambit.

I tried to explain, but it was clear Andy wanted to try before buying into the MMA ethos.

"I've done Martial Arts before. I have had loads of bare-knuckle fights, what's different here?"

My patience was running low. I was tired and hungry and ready to change from nice to nasty.

"Do you want to spar? Anything goes," I offered. His eyes lit up like I had given him the key to the sweet shop and said *help yourself*.

"Yes. Let's go."

By now, the class had cottoned-on to the situation and all eyes were upon me. We put on the only MMA gloves that seemed available back then, the infamous Harbingers, and got ready to fight. I wasn't intending to punch, after all, this little bloke didn't look like he could fight sleep. We circled a little, I moved away from his right hand, and threw a fast jab that was really a feint for the shot to take this little Jack Russell to the mat. It worked.

I moved to side control and held him, at least for a while. This guy was like a demon, moving about like his life depended on it. Like riding a bucking bronco, I was unable to keep him down and soon he got back up, like a demented Jack in the Box. He threw a hard couple of punches that I deftly blocked with my face and aimed a kick to my baby makers.

Right, enough is enough. I started throwing leather back at him, taking him down again and, this time, securing a back take. His fingers were going for my eyes. He wriggled so much that I nearly lost position, but the sweat that was pouring off us both made the choke slip in, and under, his chin. I squeezed for all I was worth, the eel-like wriggling making it more exhausting the longer we struggled.

Eventually, he stopped moving and signalled defeat. Jumping to his feet, he said, "Let's go again."

This bloke was possessed. It was obvious he loved to fight, and size, reputation, or any other factor didn't bother him. It was apparent from the next fight that his skill was on the feet. He hit hard and fast and was oblivious to pain.

The ground was his kryptonite, so again I took the fight there, although by now I was really enjoying a good stand-up scrap. Andy signed up for lessons that day, later taking over the Academy when I moved away for work reasons. He is still a Jack Russell that I would want on my side in any sticky situation, as well as a great friend.

The day a couple of Hell's Angels walked into the gym stands out vividly though. These two looked like extras from a horror movie, clad in their cut-offs and almost filling the room with their sheer size and weight.

"We want to try this grappling stuff out."

"No problem," I reply. "Do you want to take this class?"

"No. We want to fight."

Okay, here we go again. It had got to the point where I wasn't always the one to step up first. After all, I had Nige and Andy, both of whom were now capable of proving the techniques. But something made me want this one. Maybe it was the Old Mod vs Rocker thing that had laid dormant for far too long, who knows, but I accepted the challenge.

I took the first guy down without him landing a punch, mounted him, and slapped him hard about the beard until he rolled over, giving me the chance to close the choke around his huge tattooed neck. It was a good job this monster knew enough to tap-out, as I wasn't up for letting go until he was sleeping like a baby.

Biker Number 2 thought it hilarious that his mate had been manhandled so effortlessly. But, be it pride or stupidity, he wanted his chance to better me. The result was much the same only, this time, I took an Americana arm lock, wrenching hard on his arm until he verbally submitted.

After graciously taking their defeat, the hairy bikers exited stage left, declining my offer of them joining our rapidly-growing band of merry men. But, if I thought our paths would never cross again, I was mistaken.

A couple of weeks later I was out in town with a few of the lads from the gym, enjoying a cold beer, or two. We walked into a busy pub that was particularly rowdy, even for a Saturday night.

It was a proper boozer, not like these artificial pubs we have now. You could feel the atmosphere as soon as you got through the front door. Cigarette smoke cast a fog around the pub and you could taste stale woodbine in the air as you wended through the crowd to get to the bar. I had been waiting a while to get served when I felt a hand on my shoulder.

"How's it going mate?"

I turned sharply to see one of the two bikers from the challenge. My first thought was, *here we go again*. I knew that a lot of these lads carried weapons and that this could be a very different fight.

"Jonty is over there," gestured the Hairy Biker. "Come and say how-do."

"Yeah mate, let me just get a beer and I will be right over," I said.

I pushed my way through the crowd until I saw not only the two hairy bikers, but what looked like the entire Chapter of the local Hell's Angels. My mates were now with me and, although a couple had been at the gym on the day that I had fought these two headcases, most had no clue and seemed a little apprehensive.

I must admit I wasn't sure this was the best idea either as we got closer to the great unwashed. I was within touching distance when a huge roar went through the gang.

"Fucking ace what you did to these two cock jockeys," said the man I later learned was the leader of the gang. I was suddenly surrounded by a dozen leather-clad boozed-up bikers, all wanting to shake my hand. The night was to get a bit weird when several of the group wanted to feel some of the submission holds for themselves. The thought did cross my mind that maybe I had got this wrong and rather than a Biker gang, I had stumbled upon a fetish group that liked being hurt. No matter. Suffice to say, I didn't pay for another drink all night, and had a great laugh with my new leather-clad friends. I certainly have never forgotten these *nut jobs* or the hangover from Hell the day after.

But, if I thought the two bikers were the biggest lads that would challenge me, I was wrong. Around this time, I was teaching a Saturday class at Lancaster University to a small but keen group of students. We used a squash court, mostly, in the early days, that we turned into a dojo by throwing down a few judo mats.

We were well into a training session one Saturday when the squash court door opened and in walked one of the widest human beings I have ever set eyes upon. One of my students, Emmett, knew the lad and informed me that he was a UK Powerlifting Champion. He then said that this *unit* (we will call him Goliath) wanted to try MMA.

I approached Goliath and proffered a hand, which was swallowed up by his giant paw and crushed as if in a vice. "I want to see if this stuff is any good," he said.

"Okay, so, what do you want to do? Take a class?"

"No. I want to see if it can work against a non-compliant opponent."

Damn, here we go again, I found myself thinking. But, invading this thought train was one of excitement and anticipation that said, *fucking let's have it*.

There was no point in delaying. Now was the time for David to face Goliath again only, this time, David wasn't armed with a sling shot, he had something better - Jiu-Jitsu.

There was always an impending feeling in these challenges that I could end up with the crap getting royally beaten out of me in front of my students. But that was fleeting. I had a duty to prove my art. I made a quick mental calculation as we squared up: *if Goliath's gigantic fist connected with my head, I would, in all, likelihood go to sleep without the need of a bedtime story*.

Goliath looked even bigger as we circled. He had adopted an orthodox stance, which meant his power would come from the right hand. I stayed out of reach and moved in an anti-clockwise circle to avoid a collision between his right fist and my jawbone. It was obvious after a short time, me moving around him, that he was getting frustrated. I stopped suddenly, moving around him and dropping levels, then shooting forward to close distance and take his giant frame to the mat.

Great plans sometimes go awry, and this was one of those times. Usually, my shot would have lifted my opponent into orbit before bringing them crashing back down to Earth with a bang. On this occasion, I felt like one of those crash test dummies they use to test car safety in a head-on smash. Bang. I hit Goliath with the power of someone catapulted from a cannon. He didn't move.

At least, he didn't move backwards as I had hoped. Wrapping his huge arms around my waist, he lifted me into the air. My legs above, head facing the mat. With a see-saw motion, I was able to twist and turn as I sailed over his shoulder, somehow ending up on his back. To this day, I have no clue as to how, but I was in the perfect position to lock in a rear naked choke.

I secured my position by putting in my hooks (legs and feet wrapped around his legs) and began to squeeze for all I was worth. I sensed his panic. He flailed like a demon had possessed his massive frame. I could feel his body slowly surrendering to the inevitability of the choke. But he wasn't quite ready to give up. Our struggle had seen us move off the soft matted area to continue dancing on the hard, wooden floor. He knew this as he jumped into the air before crashing onto his back, crushing me under his considerable weight.

If he thought I would let go and give up, he was wrong. If he was the bullmastiff, then I was a demented Jack Russell in this dog fight, once my grip was in. I continued to squeeze even though my back felt like it was a shattered egg shell. I felt the fight slip from this behemoth and the gurgle signalled that it was over. Thank fuck.

The man mountain wanted another go. My back was in pieces having had this big lummox land on me. One of my students agreed to fight. This time, the fight plan went well and, having taken Goliath to the mat, mounted and waited until, inevitably, the big guy rolled over to expose his neck. Jiu-Jitsu guys and gals get more excited at the sight of a good neck than Count Dracula.

Anyway, Goliath never signed up for lessons, but he can probably bench press a building and has a physique that will ensure that no one ever kicks sand in his face and runs off with his girlfriend.

This episode brings me to my favourite Jiu-Jitsu statement:

"No egos in Jiu-Jitsu."

Over the years, this saying has been echoed around every Jiu-Jitsu academy that has mushroomed up since Royce Gracie popularised the art. I always illustrate my take on this saying by giving an example of how people that hold reputations as 'street fighters' get annihilated by the smallest person in the gym. And, although a Jiu-Jitsu roll is not a full-on fight where anything goes, the defeat on the mats can have one of two outcomes. Either, *Mr I'm A Streetfighter* will leave the mats never to return, or they will decide to lose their ego and learn a truly effective combat art.

As for challenges, this trend seems to have dissipated as the years have gone by. I can't think of any other Martial Art that had so much to prove than Jiu-Jitsu and MMA. I, for one, am pleased that I don't have to rep the art anymore but, strangely, I enjoyed those days and wouldn't change a thing.

It was time for a new challenge.

29

Absolute Beginners

"Only dead fish go with the flow." Unknown

My training, up to this point, was mainly No Gi Submission Wrestling and Mixed Martial Arts.

One Saturday, a new face walked into the gym and enquired about joining the class. He certainly looked the part, dressed in a long-sleeved rash guard and Vale Tudo shorts. After a brief chat, the lad introduced himself as Darren Harrop. He told me that he had trained BJJ in America and held a Blue Belt under Pedro Sauer, a respected Rickson Gracie Black Belt. To say I was excited at the prospect of rolling (live sparring) with a legit BJJ Blue Belt was an understatement.

He rolled smoothly and, although I had a few pounds on him, I was unable to catch him in any of my tried and tested subs and we fought to a stalemate. Darren was a very humble lad, and, after our roll, he invited me along to his Gi class in Blackpool the following Thursday. I was definitely up for that.

The gym that Darren was teaching out of was, for its time, an amazing space. Two floors that offered matting and punch bags, showers, and decent changing rooms. It was owned by a Kung Fu practitioner called Alan Scott who, incidentally, had the best Kung Fu I had/have ever seen. Darren was just starting to get his name out there, and BJJ was still in its infancy in the UK so the class was small. I thoroughly enjoyed the lesson and, as I hadn't worn the Kimono in a while, I found the grips and leverage so far removed from my Sub-Wrestling base. At the end of the session Darren asked if I would like to stay back and roll. This time it was a different outcome from our No Gi battle and I soon found myself sailing through the air and dumped on my back before being choked and arm-locked at will.

This was amazing. I had got used to being the big fish in the small pond I was teaching in, but now Darren made me feel like a minnow. Which was the best outcome I could have hoped for. I decided that I needed to concentrate on the Gi, as the grips it afforded were a complete game-changer. Alan asked if I would take on an MMA class at the gym, which I jumped at the chance to do, as it meant that I could continue being taught by Darren.

The gym, Kixx, was a melting pot of talent. Andy Brownbridge taught Thai Boxing, Alan was the Kung Fu teacher and myself and Darren Harrop taught the BJJ and MMA. I also met another local legend there, Paul Rice. Paul and I would go on to run our own gym for a time, and we trained together and had a good friendship. It's weird looking back on the Kixx days as I am still great friends with these lads. Strangely, the only one that doesn't train anymore and never went beyond the grade of Blue Belt in BJJ was Darren Harrop. He was an amazing coach and I took loads away from my time as his student.

Paul later got a Black Belt in BJJ and now teaches out of his own academy. Andy Brownbridge teaches K1 and Thai at my gym, and Alan now trains BJJ with me after he had to give up his beloved Kung Fu and gym for health reasons.

These were, in many respects, great days. Everyone shared knowledge, and everyone helped each other. It's amazing what you can learn from other like-minded Martial Artists. For example, Alan Scott had an amazing base, you just couldn't move him (he brings many of the aspects he learned in Kung Fu to his Jiu-Jitsu). Andy Brownbridge had trained for as long as I had and has a wealth of knowledge, and Darren had learned his art under a *bona fide* legend in Pedro Sauer. As for me, I was a brawler, desperate to hone my skills. But I was also open to learning and improving from anyone that could teach me.

Kixx was, in many respects, a true Mixed Martial Arts Academy; we had it all under one roof. I handed over my own Lancaster academy to two of my students and concentrated my efforts on spreading the word to Blackpool's finest.

30

Let It Bleed

"Next to trying and winning, the best thing is trying and failing."
LM Montgomery

The UK took a long time to host its first MMA show. People like Lee Hasdell were pioneers, founding fathers, if you will, but we were light years from landing our first man on the UFC surface, the legend that is, Ian Freeman.

Back in the day, we were more likely to fight in gyms. I had dozens of these dojo contests but *craved* the octagon. By the time our small island had its first MMA show, I was fast approaching the Big 4-0. Life, it is said, starts at 40. My life thus far had been a real humdinger. It was to transpire that my first step into a 'proper' MMA competition would be an experience I would never forget.

Myself and my then Gym partner, Paul Rice (Ricey), had signed on to fight in a *winner takes all* 8-man tournament in Birmingham. In fact, it was the brainchild of Marc Goddard, later to make his name as not only a great coach but also as a referee for the UFC. We took the challenge seriously and trained hard for the upcoming tournament. Paul had *worked the doors* in Blackpool for years and had a fearsome reputation. He also knew some of the biggest door lads I had ever seen and brought them into our training sessions. We were both Old School in our approach to training and put together a gruelling regime of sparring and body weight conditioning exercises such as Hindu squats and press-ups. But it was the sparring and live training that had onlookers shaking their heads in disbelief.

We could have opted for an easy life, beating up our students, but that's not in either of our DNA. Instead, we sparred the roughest motley crew you could imagine, as well as beating the crap out of each other. I once suffered a concussion in a rather lively exchange with Ricey. The trouble was, I didn't realise I was concussed until the drive home. I spent the night in Blackpool Victoria Hospital having a torch shone in my eyes every hour on the hour.

One of our favourite (not) training methods was to get someone to push us up against the wall mats, laying their weight on us and try to either sub us or punch us out. Now when I say these sparring partners were big, I mean BIG. I weighed in at 82kg; these monsters had at least 6 stone on me.

One of the lads was a huge Mauri called Dennis. Now, not only was Dennis ripped and heavy, but he had that instinctive *do or die* fighting spirit that is so apparent in his fellow countrymen. Dennis was tasked with holding and punching me during one particularly horrible session. His fists were double the size of mine, and boy did I feel it. The only thing I had in my favour was my Jiu-Jitsu.

In between trying to fend off Dennis' attempts to give my face a much-needed lift via his knuckles, I was trying to turn in and get back to my feet, or at least to be in a position to use a submission. I somehow managed to sink in a triangle, which Dennis saw as an opportunity to lift me into the air and smash his way out of trouble. I wasn't for letting go, like a Jack Russell clinging on to a stick. Dennis eventually succumbed to the triangle and, briefly, my stint in Hell was over. At least until we had a change of partners.

Randle was another ex-Doorman. Nice enough bloke but, like Dennis, he had an edge about him. Randle had trained in a few Martial Arts and wasn't shy of a good scrap. Unlike Dennis, Randles' Achilles Heel was his fitness. He was a nightmare for the first couple of minutes but rasping if it went longer. One of my memories of Randle during this time was him asking me to spar full-contact, without gloves. Never one to shy away from a challenge, I accepted. The state of our faces after the fight still makes me smile. I looked like I had been in a no holds barred fight with a grizzly bear. But it was fun.

Ricey and I made a good team. He was the better striker and I the more experienced grappler (nowadays it's a different story as Paul is also a BJJ Black Belt). My strategy when sparring Paul was always the same; stay away from his heavy hands, shoot in and get a submission. Things didn't always go to plan and one day I got hit with a heavy right hook that nearly had me out for the count. I somehow shook it off, but something didn't feel right. My left ear was aching like Hell.

Upon feeling for damage, I found that Paul's punch had *cauliflowered* the ear and it was filling with fluid. Damn, this wasn't good. The tournament was two weeks off. I knew a nurse and asked her to drain the ear, but every time she did, it filled up like a hot water bottle.

The day of the fight soon came around, but my ear was still bad. The fluid was still loose, and, in hindsight, I should have pulled out of the competition. But pride is a bitch that keeps nagging at your inner fears. *Don't back out. What will the team think? That you bottled it?*

I never contemplated not fighting and I was relishing the chance to fight in front of a good crowd. Upon reaching the venue and checking in, we began warming up for our first bout. I was first up. Paul was cornering me and followed me out to the Ring. I felt elated as we took the walk and my mind was racing with techniques I wanted to showcase.

My opponent was already in the ring. He was about the same size as me, younger by a good few years (I was 42 at this time) but I wasn't fazed by him. Marc Goddard called us to the centre of the ring and, after a quick reminder of the rules, we were set to fight. I didn't hesitate, coming out like a bullet and throwing a left and right combination that met their mark. My plan was to back this young gun up and then take him to the mats. Not a bad plan, as I was confident that I could beat him in a ground game.

We exchanged some heavy shots. I felt my eye start to close from a particularly heavy punch. This lad had good hands. I decided that I would chop him down with leg kicks to weaken him before my shot to take him into *my church* (the ground). I hammered his leg with inside and outside Thai kicks. I could see that his movement was slowing. He was hurt. Now was my chance.

I threw a combination of blitz punches which forced him back to the ropes. I had him in a double under clinch, perfect control from which to drop to double leg and lift him into a slam takedown. I could feel his panic. He pushed my head away with his wrists, attempting to gain distance and start punching again. His gloved hand tore the skin on my left ear - the one that looked like a Quaver crisp. I could feel his pressure so, in a quick movement, I disengaged and threw some heavy punches at him.

He covered well and circled out of the danger of having his back on the ropes. I felt a hard right-hook. I saw a waterfall of blood hit the canvas, and then I saw Marc Goddard jumping between us. Ricey jumped into the ring and told me to kneel down.

"What's up?" I asked, "It's only a bloody nose, get out of here and let me fight on."

Paul held me down and said, "Gaz, don't panic, but your ear has come off."

My first thought was, *Okay, but where is it?* It wasn't on the canvas.

"Where is the fucking thing?" I asked.

"It's still on your head, but it's hanging by a thread," replied Ricey.

"How long left in the round?" I spat.

"A minute," he replied.

"Then let me fight on."

I was obviously *talking bollocks* but, at that moment, I genuinely wanted to at least end the round. Marc gave me a towel to hold against my now very bloody head.

My initial thought was that I felt sorry for my opponent; it wasn't his fault. I truly believe I am one lucky person. The venue of the fight was less than two miles from Selly Oak hospital. This hospital is the best in the country for plastic surgery and is where our injured troops go for procedures. I was sitting in the back of the ambulance with a female technician speeding towards the hospital.

"So, am I going to lose the ear?" I asked.

"I'm not sure," the tech replied. Not the news I was hoping for.

"Oh well, I guess I will have to grow my hair to cover the hole. Maybe I can start a trend, call it the *Van Gogh*!"

Here I was, losing blood, with a real risk of losing my ear, and all I could do is joke. I often reflect on how I use humour as a mask to hide my real feelings.

Upon arrival I was prepared for emergency surgery. Long story short, my ear was sewn back on and, although it looks a mess, it still holds my glasses in place (albeit it a bit wonky). If there is any consolation, my opponent was unable to continue due to the damage to his legs from my Thai kicks (who said I'm only a grappler?) Paul fought well but was caught in a heel hook, forcing a tap-out.

The internet forums went wild with talk of the MMA fighter that had lost his ear, but I wasn't really bothered by it. I just wanted to fight again. I realise now how lucky I was to be participating in a well-run show that was overseen by a great referee. By the time I was discharged from hospital and back in Blackpool I was something of a celebrity, if only for the fact that I had wanted to continue fighting without a left ear.

One night, I was taken to a hotel in Blackpool to meet some local 'businessmen'. They had heard about my fight, and my ear getting ripped off, and were intrigued by the story. After a few drinks and piss-taking from the leader of this group of 'business associates', I was led into another part of the bar to meet someone else. I must admit, I was enjoying my fifteen minutes of fame.

Sat quietly, and looking very dapper in a grey suit, was a gentleman of, perhaps, 70 years old. He proffered a hand without speaking. He had a good grip for an elderly man and there was something in his eyes that said, "Don't fuck with me."

"Eric, this is Gaz," said the bloke that had led me to the table.

"I know about you," Eric said, in heavy London accent. "You're that fuckin' nut that had his ear ripped off and wanted to fight on."

I was dumbfounded, as I still didn't know who this man, who seemed to command the respect of everyone in the bar, was.

"Eric Mason, very pleased to meet you son. Now, will you take a drink with me?"

Jeez. Eric Mason. As in, *Kray Twins Gangster fame*. Someone I had read about in countless accounts of the infamous gangland brother's rise and fall in 60's London, wanted to have a beer with me.

We chatted for a while, Eric wanting to know the in's and outs of the fight. My now-cauliflower for an ear got prodded a lot that night, the drink flowed and, more to the point, I don't think I paid for any of them. All the lads I met that night, including Eric Mason, were great company, regardless of their reputation, and I never forgot their hospitality.

I wasn't yet done with fighting and, about a year after the ear falling off bout, I was scheduled to fight again, this time on the

Butlin Brother's Show. Ian and Andy Butlin were well known as MMA fighters and as lads you really didn't want to fall out with. In short, they were as hard as a bag of nails. Nice blokes, though, and well respected. They were a part of what was known as, 'The Northern Cartel', an amalgamation of some of the toughest gyms in the North West of England.

Along with the Butlin's team there were more great lads that fought and who were major movers and shakers in the early MMA days, such as Carl Fisher, Aaron Chatfield, Danny Rushton, Danny Wallace and a host of very able MMA fighters that seemed to be dominating the domestic circuit wherever they competed.

I was up against one of the lads from Ian Butlin's gym. Again, I gave a few years (about 15) to a younger opponent. Aaron Chatfield was refereeing and, after calling us to the centre of the octagon, we were ready to go. My opponent, Jamie Jebson, was as game as they come and, after an initial feeling-out process - eating a couple of my fists and now-reliable leg kicks – he shot in for a takedown. His speed took me by surprise and I was soon elevated and unceremoniously smashed into the canvas.

I quickly spun to pull guard, but Jamie knew that my submission game was my best offensive and stood back up. I regained my feet, disappointed that we hadn't had a chance to fight on the ground. We both traded some leather and I forced Jamie's back to the cage wall. He was strong and spun me around. I wanted him on his back, so I attempted a leg reap. Somehow, he managed to turn me, and I was the one with my back to the canvas. Jamie quickly mounted and started raining down some heavy *Ground and Pound*. I bridged and bucked, in an attempt to escape his mount, and felt happy with my attempts. The next thing I knew, Jamie was getting off me and Aaron had called the end of the fight.

"What are you doing?" I exclaimed, "I was getting out of that! You stopped the fight too soon."

Aaron looked at me and, in a calm voice said, "I saw your last fight, you had your ear torn off and wanted to continue. I have to protect fighters that don't want to quit."

His call. And I respected it, and him, but I did believe the fight could have gone on. And, I hadn't lost an ear on this occasion.

It wasn't all bad, though – Ricey had won his fight, so at least we didn't both get a loss, as in the previous outing.

The fight with Jamie was to be my last MMA bout. I decided to concentrate on my Jiu-Jitsu and running my gym. I had decided that age 43 was a little too old to be putting my body through the daily grind that is needed to get into shape for an MMA contest.

Competing in Jiu-Jitsu and No Gi submission grappling was still on the cards though. I enjoyed competition too much to stop altogether, and grappling was a bit easier on my body.

Karl Tanswell started a great competition called the Submission League. The comp was held several times a year and, much like the Football League, the more you won, the higher up the league you moved. I had some great battles, including a bout with Michael Bisping (who won on the ref's decision), but I finished the season placed Number 3 in the UK, ahead of Bisping.

My main nemesis was a wrestler from a great gym called Atherton Wrestling Club. His name was Kristian and he was of Polish origin, I believe. No matter, this lad was an animal and we always had a great tear-up. These wrestlers didn't play by the same rules as us Jiu-Jitsu people, and it wasn't uncommon to get an elbow grinding into you as both a means of torture and to escape a position. I often left the mat more busted up than most of my MMA matches (losing an ear the obvious exception), but I knew we had a good respect for each other as we always met in the final. A look between us would be enough to say, "Come on. let's see what you've learned since our last battle." And then a war would start.

The Submission League gave a platform to some great British Grappling talent. It was the first time I saw John Kavanagh (Conor McGregor's coach) in action. Suffice to say, his Jiu-Jitsu seemed on another level. Braulio Estima also showcased his incredible talent, causing a huge stir when he pulled of a flying arm bar in one of his matches. Talking of arm bars, it was around this time that I heard one of the funniest pieces of advice from someone on the sidelines, "You've got this, Tom! Do the *farm* bar."

Just goes to show how little the general populace knew about Jiu-Jitsu, unless this was a secret variation and I never knew it.

There was a great respect back in the day. Although rivalries were common, we all got on reasonably well. I had been training consistently at Defence Unlimited and had been awarded my Blue Belt under SBG Head Coach Matt Thornton when I heard that two Brazilian Jiu-Jitsu Black Belts were in the North West at a newly-opened facility called, The Wolfslair. Although I enjoyed the training in Manchester, I knew that I had to go and see what regular training under a legit Black Belt was like. This must have been around 2003 but my memory is a little sketchy.

No matter, having one Brazilian Black Belt was amazing, let alone two. Remember, at this time, being awarded a Blue Belt or even training under a Purple Belt was like finding the Holy Grail.

Pic: Ian Charlton

31

I Want to Hold Your Hand

"The key to immortality is first living a life worth remembering."
Bruce Lee

I received a phone call from my Mum one night to say that my Dad was in hospital.

She didn't seem too concerned and wouldn't go into details on the phone. I jumped straight in the car. Well, that's not entirely true. I was flat broke, so my first stop was Kixx.

Alan didn't hesitate to lend me enough money to fill the car up, an act of kindness I have never forgotten. Truth be told, I don't recall any of the journey as I was on autopilot. When I eventually arrived at the hospital, Mum was already there, sitting in a side room with my brother.

"What's happened?" I demanded.

"He just collapsed, he couldn't breathe," Mum said.

"Where is he?"

I was shown into a ward in the Intensive Care Unit where I saw my Dad, lying flat on a bed. The tubes and an oxygen mask made my heart skip in panic. "He's had a stroke," explained the doctor.

It was hard to reconcile the sight of this frail man, at the end of his life, with the man that I had always seen as indestructible. We were told to prepare for the worst, as the severity of the stroke was so bad it was a miracle that he had lived through it.

Although obviously unconscious, my Dad kept pulling the mask away from his face. I reached down and attempted to put the mask back on his face. I had, until this point, thought that my Dad would never know I was there or that my Mum had bent over him, kissed his forehead, and told him she loved him.

As my hand went towards his mouth with the oxygen mask, he grabbed my hand and playfully turned the wrist into his tried and trusted wrist lock. The very same wrist lock he had taught to a wide-eyed child, so blinded by hero worship to question his fanciful stories, all those summers ago. He didn't hurt me, he just wanted me to know that he was still my old man, and that he was still fighting. It was a final gift, and one I'm not sure that anyone else would or could understand. But it *was* a gift. The stroke might have put my Dad on his back, but this one simple act showed that he wasn't beaten.

The doctor advised us that, if my Dad did survive, then the chances were that he would be in a vegetative state unable to talk, walk, or do any of the things that made him the man he was. It was, therefore, a bittersweet blessing that in the early hours of cold November day, the man that had killed Hitler in a phone box passed away.

My Dad. Although a quiet and reflective man, had given so much to his family and he had enjoyed a very healthy life up until the stroke. I refuse to remember him in those final hours, wired up to a machine, struggling to breathe. I choose to look back to those long afternoons when he would square-up to the ten-year-old me, playfully landing a slap on my ear, before effortlessly taking the fight to the floor, his carpet slipper lightly placed across my throat, my wrist turned until I gave in. Or, the hours he would hold my attention with the wildly outlandish stories he told, painting each with colour and excitement. I thought back to a time when more life stretched before him than lay in his shadow. A strong man who placed fair play above all else.

Mum died two years later, after a courageous battle with lung cancer. In all the time she was ill, I never once heard her complain or bemoan her situation. At her funeral I read the poem 'Invictus', as it summed up perfectly how she and my Dad had lived and died.

32

Take Me To Church

"Sometimes, we can only find our true direction when we let the wind of change carry us." Mimi Novic.

News reached me that there was a Brazilian Jiu-Jitsu Black Belt just an hour away. Nothing was going to stop me now; it was as if everything up to this point had led me to here and now. If my parents passing was going to mean anything, it was that I needed to stop drinking and dedicate myself to my goal.

It wouldn't be easy. I had used alcohol as a crutch every time the proverbial shit had hit the fan before. But this time, something had changed inside me. I took a long, hard look at myself and didn't care for the reflection that bounced back. Something had to be addressed if I was going to come through this. I knew from experience that no one could make the changes needed but me. I thought about the fuck-ups that were blighting me; the inner demons that seemed to take delight in stopping me in my tracks.

It took me a while to find The Wolfslair MMA Academy. Housed on an industrial park in Widnes, the outside of the academy looked impressive, with its bold red logo above a roller shutter front entrance. I was too late for the BJJ class and, rather than upset people by walking onto the mat late, I headed upstairs to the mezzanine to watch the class.

My first impression was of how cold the building was. It was mid-winter but there seemed to be no heating other than one small gas heater next to the mat, that a man, who I assumed was the head coach, Mario Sukata, sat astride. Brazilian, built like a tank, wearing a Gi and Black Belt, whilst wearing socks (must be a Brazilian abroad thing).

The gym itself was unbelievable, a good sized industrial unit that had showers, a changing room, kitchen, a weights/cardio section and even accommodation for visiting fighters. But it was the main room that took your breathe away. The small entry door led onto a huge white mat with a red circle. The red circle was painted by Mario to cover a Gracie Barra logo that had originally adorned the centre of the mat. The walls were covered and padded in the same style. At one end of the area, a full-sized cage and boxing ring complimented the look. I had never seen anything like it. A lot of money and thought had gone into this project. Anthony and Lee, the owners, had followed their dream of building a state of the art training facility that would rival anything across the globe. They were fans of the sport and not only invested in the building but in the coaching staff too. Aside from Mario, there was a wealth of talent in the individual arts that make up MMA. So if you wanted to kick, punch, wrestle or grapple, this place was your one stop shop. Even though it had an aesthetic quality, it was also very much a 'real' fighters gym, hence the lack of heating, and blood stains on the white matting and cage and ring floors. By the time I joined the gym, a wealth of talent was emerging on domestic shows across the country with people like Alex Cook, Tom Blackledge and Michael Bisping too name a few Wolfslair *stand outs*. These young pioneers of MMA were living the dream, training full-time and guided with great management and instruction. It is little wonder that the Wolfslair became a universally respected name in the fledgeling MMA world.

The biggest shock though, was how small the Jiu-Jitsu class was. I think there were about four lads training that night. How could this be? A Brazilian Jiu-Jitsu Black Belt was in the UK, and only four people were training with him?

After the class I made my way downstairs to speak to Mario. I explained that I really wanted to train under him and his team and enquired about private lessons. I liked Mario straight away, he had a welcoming manner and friendly disposition that drew people to him. Mario listened to my nervous chatter before telling me to be at training the following night. I told him that I was a Blue Belt but that I would be happy to go back to White Belt. Mario laughed and said, "I will see how you do."

I was elated. After all the years I had spent wandering aimlessly in a Jiu-Jitsu desert I had finally found an oasis in the form of a BJJ Black Belt that was willing to teach me. If the standard of the lads I had witnessed was anything to go by, he could really help my game.

The next night I made sure I was there early. The gym was closed on arrival, but it wasn't long before the door opened, and I was greeted by Mario. That first session was amazing, albeit bloody freezing. Unlike any Jiu-Jitsu lesson I had ever been to, Mario had seamless transitions, and every technique was flawless. The rolling at the end of the class was fun too. I gassed-out a little as I had not been training as hard as usual and I was carrying a few extra pounds. Surprisingly the coldness in my bones didn't last long and I was soon in a lather of sweat, steam rising from mine and all the other heads of the small bunch of eager disciples of the class.

I felt that I performed okay over most rolls, tapping-out the White Belts, but then I was paired with Kojak, so called because of his bald head (a reference to the 70's detective of the same name). Brazilians like to give nicknames, and his was as apt as any I had heard. Kojak was on another level, although he held the same grade. He was athletic, had a better technique than me and it wasn't long before he caught me in a submission.

It didn't matter. I felt like I had won the lottery and on the long drive home, my mind raced. I had finally found a gym that taught authentic BJJ. I knew I had a long journey ahead, but I looked forward to the ride.

I decided that if I was to get better and try at least to level the score with Kojak, I needed some extra tuition. I arranged a private session with Mario every Saturday, as well as trying to get to as many sessions at *The Wolfy* as I could. I loved the Saturday lessons, although it meant getting up early and travelling the hour drive before I even stepped on the mats.

Oftentimes I would sit outside the academy waiting for Mario. He was often late but never failed to show up. The lessons sometimes stretched me beyond my capabilities. Mario would always find a way to help me grasp the techniques, and the reward at the end of the lesson was to roll with the Master himself. This usually went down two ways. Either, I would do okay and get to a good position before being swept and submitted, or I was annihilated with ease.

I began to realise that Mario would play his game just above mine. He rarely got out of first gear, but on the occasions he did, I was thrown around like a paper plane caught up in a twister. Sometimes the weekly lessons at the academy were a real MMA nerds Nirvana. People like Rampage Jackson would wander into the gym, delivering the funniest one-liners to the enthralled students. Michael Bisping was also around too, but he never really trained in the nighttime classes, at least not when I was there.

It was always a good atmosphere in the gym. Mario had brought over some of the largest Brazilian Jiu-Jitsu guys I had ever seen.

Bigfoot Silva was around during the early days, and a more intimidating man I had yet to see. He was well-named Bigfoot; his feet and hands were huge. Then again, they were in proportion to the rest of his gigantic frame. It was strange that all these well-known MMA fighters were around, but they were all respectful and decent people. Well, for the most part.

Mario was a tough coach and he didn't suffer fools. I was told that whoever rolled with Mario in the professional fighter's classes was tapped out with ease. He had been in the game a long time and had proven himself in the bare-knuckle, anything-goes tournaments that were started in his native Brazil. The young Sukata had found fame after he stepped in at short notice to fight Dan 'The Beast' Severn. The fight, on paper, should have been an easy win for Severn. He had experience, and a big weight advantage over the then 22-year-old Sukata. The fight lasted more than 40 minutes and, at the final bell, Severn's arm was raised. Even though he had lost the fight, Sukata had won a legion of fans for his die-hard approach.

The name Sukata, roughly-translated, means 'collector'. A reference to Mario's childhood hobby of collecting all manner of things. The name is also synonymous with a car crushing business in Rio and, having been on the receiving end of Mario's hold-downs is, in my view, the most apt description.

I had been training predominantly Gi Jiu-Jitsu with Mario and on occasions he would ask one of his teammates, Andrew, a fellow Brazilian and a bear of a man, to roll with me. Suffice to say, I was often mauled by Andrew who, at this time, was a Purple Belt.

One day, Mario told me to take off the Gi and roll with Andrew. We went at each other as usual, but I seemed to do better without the threat of the many Gi chokes and sweeps that are apparent with the kimono. At the end of the roll, Mario said that my *No Gi* game was much better than in the Gi. I was surprised but had to agree and, later in my training, I always seemed to do slightly better against Kojak when the Gi's came off. But I wanted to change that and make my Jiu-Jitsu Gi rolling my A-game. It took a while, but perseverance always pays off and I felt myself growing into my Blue Belt.

Training in this environment you just couldn't fail to improve. There was always something new to learn. I still recall the first time Mario taught the X guard. I could see the entry to it from half guard that he was showing, it looked straightforward enough, but could I get it? Could I fuck. Every Saturday, Mario made me keep trying it. And every Saturday I would drive home in absolute frustration. Maybe I just wasn't physically able to master this art? It wasn't just the X guard I struggled with. I was amazed at the warm-up that Kojak and the other lads did. Handstand rolls, cartwheels and other weird and wonderful movements that my rapidly-ageing body looked at and said, 'no way'. One thing I had, and still have, thankfully, is tenacity. I refused to give up on this X guard wizardry and after a few weeks I nailed it. Not only able to demonstrate it but to actually use it effectively in rolling. This was a testament to this academy, everyone wanted you to get better, especially Kojak, as the better I got, the better rolls we had. These were great sessions. One Saturday, Mario brought Ricardo De La Riva (more about him later) over to teach. I still recall being in awe of his concepts, the way he did an arm bar so that you couldn't get stacked by your opponent, or his amazing guard system. We lapped up the session, eager to learn from this great coach. I really got into my De La Riva guard after that seminar and still use it to great effect to this day. I also still teach De La Riva's concept for the arm bar. Priceless. This sort of training was worth its weight in gold.

But it was more than the techniques. The Wolfslair training was tough. From the hard warm-up we would do pass the guard, hold the guard. 5 minutes of trying to pass whilst your partner did his best to sweep you. A great way of developing your top and bottom game. After some techniques we went straight into some hard rounds of rolling. Even though the classes were quiet, we always pushed ourselves hard, and Mario was always on the mat rolling with us which was always the highlight of a class for me. It was the time that Mario would demonstrate that the technique he had just shown would work in a live situation as you were either launched by X guard sweep or subbed with ease.

My time at The Wolfslair was amongst the best times of my life. There was a real camaraderie amongst us and I looked forward to these sessions more than anything else in my weekly routine. I was still teaching in my own gym and decided to bring Mario in, once a week, to teach at my school. It was a good move, as the team went from strength to strength under Mario's guidance. The extra training helped me too and, after a couple of years, I was graded to Purple Belt.

Purple Reign

Purple belt was a major milestone in my BJJ journey. At first, like anyone that attains a new grade, I just didn't feel ready to rep the belt. But, with time, you grow into your new grade. This was a major time of development for my BJJ. I loved to play guard, especially De La Riva, but I also wanted a good top game and had to work hard to develop this aspect. I had some good students, but I was the highest grade at my gym. At the Wolfy, it was still me and Kojak going through the belts together, but there were some tough blue belts snapping at our heels.

I felt a huge pressure with the colour Purple. I suppose ego can be a problem as no one wants to get tapped out by a lower belt. The step up from Blue to Purple belt is huge. Remember, back in the day a blue belt was a rarity, so tying this new belt around my waist each time I stepped onto a mat felt at odds to me. I started to analyse the belts in BJJ and how they equate to skill. I figured that at the white belt stage we are mostly survivors, doing anything possible to get out of the water without a shark taking your arm home with it. The white belt is the sponge stage where, if you are in the right environment, you will learn a wealth of great concepts and techniques. Of course, the white belt stage typifies the 'hammer and nail' period. Usually when you start you are the nail, being hit from all angles by the hammer (the more experienced). Eventually, you will start to hit the odd nail yourself, when the handful of techniques that you know start to pay out like a faulty one-armed bandit. With each stripe on your white belt the confidence is beginning to show. You might even be that most valued white belt that coaches others, usually during a roll, and usually when you are just about to be tapped out. Oh, how the coaches love a good white belt sensei.

At Blue belt, you have started to grasp the arts' nuances. I often liken the development of Jiu-Jitsu to that of learning to read and write. When we first start training, we are unable to read. We can see the letters, but they make no sense. As we continue on our education, we start to learn the alphabet of Jiu-Jitsu. But still, we are unable at this stage to put the letters found within, to make or form a word. We continue to learn, and soon simple words are absorbed. Think scissor sweep into mount. This is our most basic 'Cat' and 'Dog' in terms of words we now understand and can write. Further down the line, we can not only form words but have learned sentence structure. Think Blue belt. After you have developed your 'reading and writing', you are able to write your own story. This is when your Jiu-Jitsu is a language tool. You are able to dictate what you want to do. You have become educated in this great art. It is now up to you, and the talent you have, as to how far you can take these newly acquired literary skills. At the highest echelon in Jiu-Jitsu, Helio Gracie is our version of Shakespeare. He has not only written the classics but has introduced new vocabulary that we now all use in our day to day practice. But, like Shakespeare, many great writers have followed. In our art, Rickson Gracie, the Mendes brothers, and a host of talent continue to push boundaries, and this makes for a never-ending story.

Anyway, here I was at purple belt, able to put together a few good sentences but still learning, not yet ready to write the book. In terms of my Jiu-Jitsu journey, purple belt was to prove my most successful grade. And, in many respects, was also when I really started to understand the complexity of this great art. The real skill in Jiu-Jitsu is to always stay in the mindset of the student. We can learn from anyone. But the main thing to grasp is that it doesn't matter who you can beat on the mat. If you can't beat yourself, get rid of limiting factors such as ego, you will never reach your potential.

33

Heroes

"Heroes may not live long in years, but they live forever in the stories." Amit Kalantri

Mario asked if Kojak and I were up for a trip to Rio, where we were to train and compete in the International Masters and Seniors BJJ Championships.

It was 2009. I was doing well in my day job and had a few quid saved, so it was a no-brainer for me. The day of the trip arrived, and I drove down to Warrington to meet Kojak and Mario. We took a taxi to Manchester Airport, checked-in our baggage and waited for our flight. We were all in great spirits, excited about the adventure that lay ahead.

We had settled into some comfy seats with a brew and a sandwich and waited for our flight to be announced as ready to board. We eventually got a bit twitchy as the time of the flight departure had come and gone. We approached the BA flight desk and enquired as to the hold up and were staggered to be told that we had missed the flight. How could this be, we demanded, as no notification had been given? We were told that, to the contrary, our names had indeed been called, several times, and when we had not turned up, our bags had been taken off the plane.

We were devastated and asked if there was a chance of getting a later plane. The airline staff told us, much to our dismay, that there was no chance and the only thing we could do was to buy another ticket. We considered every option, from getting a taxi to London and joining our flight there, to counting our losses and going home. There was no chance that I was missing the trip to the home of my beloved art. I took out my credit card and booked us all on a new flight. It was expensive, but I had the money, and Mario and Kojak agreed that we should go. They would pay me back when we got home.

Tickets bought, we made sure we were the first in line to board the plane and, at last, we were on our way. The plane journey went smoothly and without incident. Mario and I sat on one side of the plane whilst Kojak sat huddled up next to one of the largest human beings I had ever seen. We were in fits of laughter when we heard the *man mountain* ask about Kojak's cauliflower ears, "Rugby?"

"No," came a squeaked reply, "Jiu-Jitsu."

Mario and I laughed all the way to Rio, but I'm not sure my squashed teammate saw the funny side. No matter, we were soon in Brazil, the home of Jiu-Jitsu. The adventure had begun.

We checked into our hotel overlooking the beautiful Copacabana beach. The weather was hot but overcast, and we could just see the statue of Christ the Redeemer through the clouds, a magnificent sight to behold. Rio is a paradox; the opulence of the beach front is overlooked by the poorest and most desolate of Rio's inhabitants who reside in the many *favelas*. The streets that wind away from the beautifully kept beachfront are a real eye-opener, and you witness poverty in its most brutal of forms.

I saw a child, no more than six years old, lying prone on the paving stones. As I bent over to help him, Mario grabbed my arm, pulling me away, "Gario, leave the boy, there is nothing you can do for him. If you give him money, he will pull out a gun and shoot you where you stand."

I was appalled that a society could allow this and, worse still, turn a blind eye to it. On the surface, the city is perfect; a playground for the rich and famous, but scratch just below the surface and you will see a poverty trap that holds its inhabitant's captive. The only hope for many is through a life of crime, selling drugs, robbing the tourists, and generally living a deprived existence in their favela fortresses that keep them safe from police intervention. It's a reality check, and hard for a Westerner to come to terms with. It shows that we are polar opposites in terms of our experiences.

Poverty is abundant across the globe, but I hoped that I would never be so used to this level of suffering that I would just walk past, never glancing or trying in some way to help another human being. There wasn't anything I could do for these poor street urchins. As Mario said, it was a desperate plight and these children were already savvy and willing to do whatever it took to survive. Their childlike innocence a mere shadow of its former self, if ever it was so.

After a quick tour of Rio, in which Mario took us to see Carlson Gracie's academy, or at least what we could see past the huge door that guarded its entrance, we headed to De La Riva's place. We planned to train at De La Riva's gym for the duration of our stay.

(Master Ricardo De La Riva is a black belt, renowned for his creation of a guard system that carries his name and is suited to his small stature. He is, however, more than just the creator of the De La Riva guard, having competed at the highest level under the legendary Carlson Gracie team and holding victories over Royler Gracie and other notable Jiu-Jitsu illuminati. De La Riva was introduced to Jiu-Jitsu after he got into an altercation on Copacobana beach. De La Riva's father was a fan of Carlson Gracie and enrolled his then 15 year old son onto a Jiu-Jitsu program in a bid to toughen him up. Known affectionately as "The 'Scientist" for his ground breaking development of modern Jiu-Jitsu, De La Riva continues to push the BJJ envelope.)

That first walk to the Equipe Gym that was host to De La Riva's academy, was a real eye-opener. At first, I thought I was imagining it but, as we walked the back streets of Rio, I realised I was not imagining the sound of cars hooting their horns, and the furtive glances from passers-by. Soon, my suspicions were founded. The Rio natives had recognised our teacher. I knew that he was quite well known, but to this extent I had no clue. Grown men were stopping him in the street. It was like being in the company of David Beckham in the UK.

Once in the dojo it was further apparent that Mario was considered something of a local legend. He was soon surrounded by fellow Jiu-Jitsu practitioners, all eager to have their picture taken with him. Mine and Kojak's faces must have been a picture. We really hadn't expected this kind of idolatry, after all, to us, he was just Mario, the bloke that kicked our asses on the mats three or four times a week.

The Mario thing was not our only shock. We stood aghast as onto the mat walked one after another Black Belt. There must have been 15 at least. We had never seen that many Black Belts in our entire time training, let alone all in one room. In fact, the lowest grade on the mat was us, two blokes from England, unable to understand a word that was being spoken, but fully comprehending the international language of Jiu-Jitsu.

Sometime later, Master Ricardo De La Riva walked into the room. This man exuded a confidence and presence I had never seen until this day. He walked up to every student, shaking each and everyone's hand, before kneeling in front of the class and taking us through a stretch before instructing us to roll. There was to be no technique section of the class, we were, after all, there to train hard for the upcoming competition. Whilst we partnered up with one of the many Black Belts, De La Riva went over to say hello to his former teammate, Mario.

As predicted, the rolls were tough, but both Kojak and I were doing well against our new sparring partners. At one point, I hit my trademark *omoplata sweep* on a young Black Belt and afterwards I excitedly recounted my move to Kojak who, at the same time, was telling me how well he had done. Mario came over and told us off for mouthing-off, basically.

Anyway, over the next few rolls I was rolled-up and dispatched by almost all my opponents. It was a humbling experience, but neither Kojak or myself meant it in a disrespectful way. We were just over-excited to finally be rolling with these awesome practitioners. The two-hour session flew by and I had certainly felt it. The heat was something I was unused to for a start, then there was the fact that, for two hours, I had only rolled with Black Belts.

We came out of the gym into the glorious Brazilian climate. I was so dehydrated I felt like I would pass out if I didn't get a drink. Mario suggested that we try an Acai. I had no clue what Acai was but, *when in Rome*, and all that.

The taste was unbelievable. The first mouthful caused a brain freeze, but I was hooked from that moment. What I thought was ice cream was, in fact, a berry indigenous to the rainforests of Brazil. Whatever it was, it did the trick. Couple this with the fact that I had just finished my first Jiu-Jitsu class in the country of its inception, I had a rush of energy and felt like I could take on the world.

After a trip to a restaurant that night, where I saw my two travelling companions almost eat their body weight in a vast selection of meats, we headed back to the hotel for an early night. As I looked out of our open balcony window at the statue of Christ looking over this city, as rich as it was poor, I remembered the little boy laid prone on the Rio streets. I wondered what his future would hold, and if he even had a future in this vast and unforgiving city. If that statue had any power or a landline to God, I hoped that it would help the boy and the thousands like him that lay in its shadow. Sleep didn't come easy that first night.

The next day I was awake early. We were heading to training in the morning session. I presumed, as it was a working weekday, that the mats would be quieter. How wrong I was. If anything, there were more Black Belts than the previous day. Furthermore, there was a film crew awaiting the arrival of Mario. After a brief interview and some techniques, the film crew left us to our training.

If I thought yesterday was hard, it was nothing compared to the morning session. The mats were soaked with sweat as we left to shower, complete with new aches and pains to add to yesterday's injuries. The shower at Equipe, or at least the one that I chose, was cold. So cold, in fact, that it took your breath away. But after you got used to it, the cold water was most welcome as it helped with the injuries.

After the cold shower it was time to refuel and for me it was to be Acai, my new food of choice. A little R&R was in order, so we decided to find a cafe nearer to the beach, and what better way to chill than by laying on those golden sands. We navigated through the streets, chatting happily as we walked. One of the things that I really liked about the lifestyle in Rio was the sight of young and old running, cycling or just working out on the beach. The locals didn't seem to care what they looked like, exercise was a way of life for these people. I particularly liked to look for those wearing Jiu-Jitsu or MMA t-shirts.

As we made our way to the beach, I spotted a man sitting at an outside cafe. Nothing unusual in this, but I noticed as we drew nearer that he was wearing a Rickson Gracie t-shirt. A little closer still, I saw that he was also wearing a Rickson Gracie cap. I excitedly got Mario and Kojak's attention.

"Hey, that bloke must train with Rickson, he's wearing the full outfit."

We were almost at the café when I exclaimed, "Mario, that *is* Rickson Gracie."

Lunch destination changed, as we grabbed the seats next to the greatest Jiu-Jitsu practitioner of our times.

People say you should never meet your heroes, the inference being that they never quite live up to expectations. I suppose it can be true that we build up an image in our heads as to what the person is like. We are only seeing the side of the celebrity that they want us to see, the *warts and all* view is usually reserved for their nearest and dearest. Anyway, I digress. Rickson turned out to be everything, and more, than I expected, although I did think, "I thought you would be taller."

On reflection, Rickson's stature was larger than life. He exuded a magnetism that made you comfortable in his presence. Kojak and I let Mario do the initial introductions. After the perfunctory hello's, Rickson went out of his way to talk to us. We must have looked a motley crew, a 6'4" Brazilian and his two pale Northern English students. Rickson was happy to talk to us for the whole of a rather nice and healthy lunch. He even saw off a beggar that was trying to get us to part with a few Reals. And, although my Portuguese was limited to *Obrigado* and *Amigo*, I could tell that he was being decent with the poor fellow. This feeling was reinforced when he offered the beggar the rest of his meal.

We wanted to ask this great man all about his philosophies and training in Jiu-Jitsu but, in the end, he ended up intrigued by our story. Mario got Rickson's email address and spoke about the possibility of him coming to the UK. Rickson was up for it and expressed a wish to see the United Kingdom. Rickson told us that he had been in Rio training his son, Kron, at his brother Royler's academy. After what seemed all too brief a time, Rickson said that he had to go, but not before my friend Kojak insisted that he bought his lunch. After a bit of persuasion, Rickson agreed to Kojak's hospitality and following a quick photo, disappeared into the crowds of Rio.

It was a while before any of us could speak. Even Mario was star struck, saying that he had always wanted to meet Rickson and that this trip was a dream come true. I broke the spell by asking the rather obvious question, "If you were the most famous Jiu-Jitsu person in the world, would you really need to have your name all over your clothing?" Just a thought. I was destined to meet the great man again a few years later at the ADCC in Nottingham. Not surprisingly, he didn't remember me. Oh well, there aren't many that can say they ate lunch with Rickson, and no matter that Rickson probably had this sort of hero worship wherever he went, for two Northerners and a bloody big Brazilian, we would always have the memory of meeting Rickson in Rio 2009.

Our time in Rio had been geared towards one thing - competing in the International Masters and Seniors BJJ Tournament. And that time was upon us.

Pic: Ian Charlton

34

Sittin' On Top Of The World

"Be wary of an old man in a profession where men usually die young." Anon.

The Tijuana Stadium is the most famous venue for BJJ tournaments in the world. And here I was, ready to compete in the biggest competition of my life. Eduardo Telles and Mike Fowler walked past me on their way to compete. It was like a *Who's Who* of Jiu-Jitsu royalty. No pressure then.

Kojak was first up and, after dominating his first opponent, his hand was raised as the victor. His next two fights went the same way and he was soon taking his place on the winner's podium. I was elated, my voice was rasping from all the shouting I had done, but what an achievement, a UK Purple Belt Masters and Seniors Champion. To add to the celebration, Mario tied a Brown Belt around Kojak's waist. To say this was an emotional sight does not do it justice. Here I was, witness to my friend and training partner's finest hour.

My name was eventually called, but soon it became evident that I was the only one in my category. Mario spoke to the officials and I was moved into the age group below, albeit a weight class above, mine. No matter, I had come to fight. There was only one other Gringo in the holding pen, a huge American who told me that he was the defending champion. He also said that it would be me and him in the first fight. The inference was that the locals wanted one of us out of the running. I didn't want to believe this, but when his name was called to the mat and, seconds later, my name was called, it made some sense.

As soon as we gripped-up I felt the weight advantage. This bloke was as strong as an ox. I broke his grips and went for a shoot takedown. The American stuffed the shot and ended up on my back. I spun into half guard, but this behemoth was forcing his way past my lock down and soon his pressure saw him take side control. Kojak and Mario were right next to the mat, and I could hear their advice as clear as a bell. The problem was that I was unable to move. I realised that I was going to lose this bout, but I was determined that he would not sub me in gaining the victory.

For the remaining few minutes of the bout he tried everything. At one point, he had a tight choke that almost saw me taking a nap in this most famous arena in the world. Somehow, I fought out of the choke and, hearing Mario shouting down the time, I decided to go hell for leather and get out of this most uncomfortable position. Just as the referee called time, I got back to my guard. I was totally spent. The American offered his hand and pulled me to my feet.

I was devastated. I felt as if I had let Mario and Kojak down. There would be no Brown Belt for me today, or the thrill of the medal on the podium.

Mario was next up. As he walked across the mat, you could hear the crowd swell with excitement. The Gracie Magazine photographer ran the length of the room to get a picture of *Sukata* and the bleachers emptied as people ran towards the mats to get a view of this legendary fighter.

My job was to shout out the time, and it was as if every time I gave an update on time remaining, Mario would move to a better position. He breezed the first bout, winning on points. His next bout saw him pull off one of the best submissions I had ever seen in a competition when he locked in a belly down armbar that nearly saw him bringing the poor unfortunate's arm back to the UK as a souvenir.

The final bout was called. Mario's opponent was the man mountain called 'Monstro'. I must admit, I had some reservations, as the weight advantage seemed huge. I needn't have worried as Mario took the fight to Monstro from the first command to engage. Another Gold medal was ours, and all that was left now was for us to celebrate.

Although I was upset that I didn't get the Gold, I was still happy that my two friends had done so well. For my part, I had loved the experience and wasn't going to be crying into my beer. We started our celebrations with some food before taking in a few bars. My last memory of this most memorable of nights is of Mario almost carrying me and Kojak back to our hotel down the beautiful Copacabana beach front. The hangover the next day was horrific, but what a great experience we had shared.

We had a few days left and, after taking the long trek up to the statue of Christ the Redeemer, looking out over the paradox of poverty and riches that is Rio, it felt like we were standing on top of the world.

35

Pride

"Gold medals aren't really made of gold. They're made of sweat, determination, and a hard-to-find alloy called guts." Dan Gable

Once home, I was determined to get straight back into competitive mode, and soon Mario asked if I was up for competing in the European Championships that were to be held in Switzerland. I had never been to Switzerland, so it was another no-brainer really.

Mario stepped up our training. We were to be accompanied on this trip by another couple of lads, Jay and Big Tony. I didn't know these lads before the trip, but it was evident from the start that we would have a laugh. I had managed to get a full sponsorship deal which covered my flights, hotel, food and entrance fee, so there was some pressure to perform well. We landed and were soon en route to our hotels, passing through the most beautiful countryside.

We only had a few days in Switzerland, so sightseeing had to be done *on the fly*. After checking into our hotel, we ventured out for food. Well, the others did. I was cutting weight and could only eat a few leaves, washed down with water. To say it felt like torture was an understatement, as Mario and the others were on weight or below weight.

The day of the competition was soon upon us and, after a short train journey, we arrived in the town that would be host to the competition. I felt good as I walked to the sports arena with Mario and my new friends, Jay and Tony. The competition was rammed. There were representatives from some of the most famous academies around the world, and the atmosphere was electric. We registered, and I was again disappointed to learn that there was no one in my age group. The organisers were accommodating and moved me into a younger bracket as had happened in Brazil a month earlier. Only this time, it was at my fighting weight. I had no issues against younger opponents, and the fact that I wouldn't be squashed and squeezed, as had happened in Rio, was a bonus. Once in my Gi, I headed straight to the warm-up area.

After a few light rolls and stretches, I headed back to watch my new friends. Jay was up first and took the Silver medal. Tony, the biggest lad amongst us, easily dominated his division and took the Gold medal. And then it was my turn.

I strode onto the mats feeling confident in my preparation and training. I was the underdog, an older competitor going against the young guns. In a way, it took the pressure off me and I was determined that I would do better than my last outing. My opponent was bouncing up and down in front of me, a Rickson Gracie badge giving away his lineage, but it wasn't going to faze me. I was a Mario Sukata Purple Belt, no one was going to walk over me this time.

After the initial fist-bump we were good to go. I pulled guard, breaking his posture, and started to attack his collar for a Gi choke. My opponent was no slouch and easily defended the attack. Gripping his right wrist and pushing his arm inwards, I jumped my legs up, locking them into a triangle. Reaching for my ankle, I pulled the left foot tightly under my right leg and squeezed. I knew I had this. Once my triangle was in, it was in. It was now just a matter of waiting for either the tap-out or for this bloke to pass out. He tapped. I could hear Mario and the lads cheering as I stood, my arm raised in victory.

One fight at a time was my plan. Don't think about the Gold medal, just get through one opponent at a time. My next fight was soon called and as I walked out of the bullpen my heart was beating so hard, I felt sure that everyone could hear it. I had watched my opponents first fight and he seemed content to play it safe and go for points. I really detested this type of game. Usually, after securing the first points, the player would hold position for as long as possible before transitioning to another hold down. Nothing wrong in this strategy, so long as a submission was the ultimate goal. Sadly, it often wasn't. My game was always about ending the fight as quickly as possible by way of tap-out. I knew this bloke had pulled guard in his first bout, so I decided to get there first. We slapped hands, bumped fists and got into our positions.

The fight to dominate grips was a quick affair. As soon as I had my grips, I put my right foot onto his hip and fell back into guard. I could feel that this was going to be a good bout. Neither wanted to give an inch. The referee circled waiting for one of us to make a move. My plan was to break down the posture. I pulled open the Gi and wrapped it around my opponent's shoulder. It did the trick. In what seemed like panic, my opponent used his strength to pull back into a better posture. It was all I needed.

As he started to push back, I swung my hips out and locked in a straight arm bar. It was one of those submissions that you knew instinctively was a fight ender. Raising my hips and pulling the arm tight, I could feel the arm popping, but something was stopping this bloke tapping. I could hear Mario shouting to go belly down to get a better leverage and that's what happened. One last push of the hips and pull of the wrist caused a snapping sound and a tap on my leg signalled that the bout was over. My opponent was writhing in agony on the mat and, for a moment, I felt bad for him. The fact was that he should have tapped sooner. There was no way he was getting out of the arm bar.

I walked over to the timekeeper's table and asked how many more fights there were to get me to the medals. His reply of, "That's it, you're in the Final," set my heart racing again. Could this be it, my time to be a winner on this great stage?

I refused to get over-confident. I still had one more fight after all. I was eager to see who my last opponent would be, and I didn't have long to wait. The fight that would determine who I would meet in the Final was a quick and one-sided affair. A kimura put an end to someone's dream and set up my bout with the lad that had secured it. I should have felt the same nerves that had accompanied my other bouts leading up to this moment, but they had mysteriously gone. It felt strange but, in my mind, I already knew I was going to win.

After the customary hand slaps, we went at it. I found myself on my back, playing open guard. My opponent circled before attempting a leg drag pass. I didn't allow him to dictate the space and quickly regained guard. It was at this point that I looked into my opponent's eyes. I could tell that he was desperate to get the win but, without even thinking, I pushed in one of his wrists and, jumping my legs high, sunk in my favourite sub, the Triangle Choke.

It was tight. I was already celebrating my Gold medal in my head. A quick tap signalled the end and I rolled over my shoulders and got to my feet. I extended a hand towards my fallen foe, helping him to his feet. We hugged, and the ref brought us to the centre of the mat, raising my arm in victory. I stood on the podium, the Gold medal around my neck. To let the crowd know who I repped, I held a large Mario Sukata back patch aloft.

My competition wasn't over just yet, though. I had decided to go for Double Gold and entered the absolutes. Tony, my new mate, was winding me up about the size of the blokes in my bracket. He had a point; I was the smallest in there. No matter, this was going to be fun. My opponent was called first, a huge Polish guy who seemed to be chiselled out of stone. I walked onto the mat behind him. I could hear Tony shouting from the balcony and looked up to see him and Mario. To this day I'm not sure what made me do it, but I blame Tony. My giant Polish opponent was still facing the opposite direction as I stood on one leg, raising my arms in a crane-style Karate Kid pose, the same one I had replicated many years before in the night club fight with the Pitt lads. It hadn't worked well for me then, so God knows why I thought this time would be different.

Tony certainly appreciated my comedy act. Unfortunately for me, the Polish behemoth didn't seem to see the funny side of things as he suddenly spun around to be confronted with my poorly-timed piss take. Let's just say that his initial attack was brutal.

Shooting in, he lifted me like a rag doll before smashing me into the tatami. I felt my skeleton rattle as I scrambled to get into guard. The giant was standing in my closed guard. Gathering my kimono, he pushed it against my windpipe, trying to choke me out. I knew I had one chance, an arm bar. Throwing my leg around his tree trunk arm and pushing my hips towards the ceiling, I could hear Mario and Tony shouting, "You've got him!" but that was the last sound I heard before being helped off the mats.

It transpired that the ref had decided to call an end to my Double Gold dream. No matter, I had come to fight, and that is what I had done.

Celebrations started as soon as we got back to the hotel. I needed to go shopping for some hair gel as, in my haste to pack, I had forgotten mine. Tony came with me to a local chemist. I headed to the counter with my 'hair gel', just wanting a quick purchase, shower and then to get out on the beers with the team. The product chosen, I walked to the counter. I could hear Tony laughing behind me but paid no heed. It was only when he said, "Gaz, that's not hair gel," that I looked at the tube in my hand.

'Veet'. If I had put this on my head, I would have soon gone as bald as my teammate, Kojak. Tony still says to this day he wishes he had let me buy the Veet. It had been a great trip and, once back in the UK, Mario gave me my Brown Belt. This was the icing on the cake.

European Champion and now a Brown Belt.

36

Somewhere Over the Rainbow

"You need to spend time crawling alone through shadows to truly appreciate what it is to stand in the sun." Shaun Hick

I continued to train hard for the next two years, making the two-hour round trip to Widnes as well as training every other day at my own gym.

One hot June evening I got a call from Mario. He told me that he had to return to Brazil and that he didn't know when, or even if, he would return. I was devastated. This man who had taught me so much, a man I was proud to call both my teacher and friend, was not going to be around anymore. Mario said that there would be a huge get-together at The Wolfslair the following Thursday and that he wanted all his students there. This was a no-brainer. There was no way I was missing this last class.

The night of the class was soon upon us. I travelled up to Widnes with a few of my students in tow. When we walked through the gym doors, I was shocked to see a mat full of students. People had travelled far and wide to train and the atmosphere was electric. The class was something of a blur, but I recall it went fast. The last half an hour or so was reserved for rolling, but tonight something was different. Instead of being told to find a partner, Mario called Kojak and myself to the centre of the mat.

We looked at each other, not knowing what was about to go down. We had rolled on these mats many times over the years, but this felt different. Mario hand-picked our rolling partners and set us off with the command, "Let's roll."

The first few rolls felt good, but it soon became evident that we were being *shark tanked*. There was no rest between rounds, and the calibre of opponents was going up every time that Mario called change. I can't speak for Kojak, but I was absolutely knackered after about 30 minutes of high-octane rolling. It was some relief when Mario called time and we were instructed to line up in belt order. The room was full of Blue and Purple Belts, but only Kojak and I wore the Brown Belts that put us at the end of the line-up.

Mario, usually very reserved and not prone to making speeches, started talking to the group. He recalled his first few classes at The Wolfslair, about how cold he had found the gym and how the BJJ classes had grown over the years. I was dripping in sweat and still breathing heavily when he called for Anthony, The Wolfslair owner, to come onto the mats. Mario called my name and, as I walked towards him, he was handed a Black Belt from Anthony.

I stopped in my tracks. The room erupted in cheers and clapping, but I was frozen to the spot. Mario took off my Brown Belt and tied the Black Belt around my still sweat-soaked waist. I think I mumbled a sort of speech, but I really don't recall much of what was coming out of my mouth. I felt a mixture of happiness and sadness as I hugged my teacher. Kojak was called next and his reaction was similar to mine. I got the Black Belt seconds before Kojak, but I always regarded him as my better in terms of skill and training time. It didn't matter to us, we had been on the same journey and now we stood before our own students and friends as Black Belts in BJJ. But more, we were Mario Sukata's first British Black Belts.

The year was 2011. My journey had started over 15 years earlier. I thought back to the early days in the UK when there wasn't even a Blue Belt on these shores. We had come such a long way in terms of the UK BJJ scene, but it was still very much in its infancy. There was so much potential for further growth in this great art. By 2011, there were perhaps 30 English-born BJJ Black Belts, I was proud to be amongst the first and prouder still that my promotion had come from a living legend, Mario Sukata.

As I looked across this packed mat, I remembered the first day I had walked through the doors as a Blue Belt under Matt Thornton. How I was amazed that this awesome teacher was teaching only four people and how, after my first lesson, I had offered to remove my Blue Belt and start afresh as a White Belt.

The Black belt is synonymous with becoming a teacher of Martial Arts. I had been teaching Jiu-Jitsu since Blue belt due, in the main, to there being no higher grades at that time. These days, with the phenomenal BJJ growth that has occurred in the UK, Blue belt teachers are now a rarity. Teaching Jiu-Jitsu is an art in itself. You might be an absolute beast on the mat but if you are unable to explain to your student base a technique or a principle, then all you will ever have in your academy is a mat full of cannon fodder. At Black belt you should also have a good understanding of how to teach. But just using the 'watch me and copy' style of instruction is like writing a poem without punctuation, it just won't have the meaning, flow or feeling that it needs to be appreciated. You need to articulate as effortlessly as you can physically demonstrate. "A teacher is a compass that activates the magnets of curiosity, knowledge, and wisdom in pupils." Eva Garrison

When I first started teaching, I only had a handful of techniques available. I had watched the content of "Gracie Jiu-Jitsu Beginner to Intermediate" so many times I thought I really understood the moves. And yes, in the gym I was able to hit the new techniques with relative ease, but that was mainly because I knew slightly more BJJ than the guys I was rolling with. As the saying goes, "In the kingdom of the blind, the one-eyed man is king." But I failed to see and understand some of the nuances that made the technique work. I was too focussed on the end result, the tap-out. Rickson Gracie talks about *invisible Jiu-Jitsu*, but I believe there is also *blinkered Jiu-Jitsu*, the exact opposite of Rickson's philosophy. In terms of my early Jiu-Jitsu experience, I was the one-eyed man. To fully appreciate Jiu-Jitsu as an art, we need to see it as it was intended, as a functioning and efficient combat system. But we shouldn't fail to see the aesthetic quality that is inherent. Jiu-Jitsu is, after all, a beautiful thing to behold. If your idea of Jiu-Jitsu is all about crushing and squeezing the life out of your opponent, then you are missing the big picture. The journey is as enjoyable as the destination. In other words, I love the whole process of catching the arm bar, not just the end result. It is a true thing of wonder as each movement brings you to the point whereby you are hyper-extending someone's arm and they are so trapped and incapacitated that the only option is to tap out. Bruce Lee said, "A punch is not just a punch, and a kick is not just a kick.". Look for the beauty in the art, that's why it is called art.

Nothing New Under The Sun

Every Martial Art, regardless of origin, will have some commonality to another. For example, the principles found in BJJ, such as distance management, having a strong base, relaxation and control are also prevalent in other systems such as Karate, Judo, Western and Thai Boxing and Kung Fu. I spoke in an earlier chapter about one of my students, Alan. Alan was an incredible Kung Fu teacher. His base and, in turn, the way that he could move you off of your base was dynamic. Now, due to injury he has switched to BJJ. The understanding that Alan has of the core principles found in his Kung Fu training are transferable skills that he has brought to his

BJJ game. He has had to be a free thinker in order that he can work around some rather serious injuries.

I also have some interesting talks with one of my other students, Mark Hodgson. Mark is an incredible Karate teacher (he would have no problems using his Karate in a phone box). We talk about the similarities that are inherent in Karate and BJJ. I'm not talking about kicking and punching, but more the stances we use, take the Standing Guard passing position in BJJ and think Horse Stance in Karate, legs stretched and knees bent for base. A low centre of gravity. At first, it is all too easy to look but not actually see. When you really start to scrape away at the surface you will find some amazing things that you might have missed. Speak to other martial artists; I can learn so much from a ten minute chat with Alan or Mark about what it is that they bring from another system. Don't just blindly think that one system has it all. These systems have been around a long time and have so much to teach. And importantly, these coaches have taught for a long time and know how to get across to an absolute beginner how and why a technique works.

For me, black belt was my time to really start 'teaching'. I had a plan that I wanted to follow. That being, giving the student as much guidance as they needed to grasp a technique. It was also around this time that I stopped using the term, 'Basics'. My students will tell you that I do not believe there is a basic technique, but rather a set of principles that are found in each technique that make it effective. We have already touched on these principles, distance management, base etc. But, in addition, I have always liked the theory of connection. Without connection, our ability to make a technique work will be diminished considerably. Think in terms of the Mount position. Without the correct control, you are not able to hold your position or, importantly, use a technique from it in order to submit your opponent. The way that we use the hips, control the head and legs and maintain balance is connection. As for 'basics', I get why a lot of instructors use the term for arm bars, scissor sweeps etc, but there is nothing 'basic' about making these techniques work. If on day one of your training I showed you a berimbolo sweep, (to many, a complex move), and explained in detail how and why it worked until you could do it without thinking, does that qualify it as a basic technique because that is what you learned first? One of the reasons we teach in the way that we do is to illustrate the core concepts of the art. The hip escape, for example. This is a move that is found in a multitude of techniques, but can it be described as basic? We see many beginner classes following a set criteria: hip escape, take down, scissor sweep, Kimura, arm bars etc. But, to an absolute beginner there is nothing basic about these techniques. These are preferred techniques to teach because of their value as a high percentage move. Take the arm bar as an example. The arm bar can be utilised from almost any position in BJJ, Mount, side control, back take and half guard. It is a high percentage sub, so it makes sense to teach it at the start of the students learning journey. The hip escape is another example. It is used both offensively and defensively. But the term basic, is misleading and doesn't do justice to the 'genius' of the art. The way that we teach a technique is also an area for debate. Some coaches show a move a few times and then allow a period of drilling. This is fine. However, we need to understand, as teachers, that people learn in different ways. Some respond to visual and some to auditory command. Everyone is different. We have different body shapes and sizes. The idea that *one move works for all* is wrong. We must adapt the techniques to fit the student, or at least help them to figure out a way that best suits them.

Teaching Jiu-Jitsu gives me more pleasure than competing ever did. Don't get me wrong, I loved to compete, but it is the relaying of information, of getting the best out of another person, that is what I love to do. Jiu-Jitsu has the power to change lives. It did mine. Jiu-Jitsu is something that transcends just the physical aspects that are apparent. In fact, all Martial Arts have this ability. I see people that have absolutely chaotic lives. They go through so much pain and heartache, but the time they spend on the mat is a release. A *moving meditation*, if you like. But more than just its huge physical and mental health benefit, Jiu-Jitsu is a bridge between all social classes, breaks down stigma, inequality and refuses to accept perceived difference of any kind. We are all the same on the mats, the only thing that separates us is the colour of the belt we wear, and even that is there for the taking, an achievable goal for all.

There had been many memorable experiences over the years but at this moment I knew that, in reality, my learning was only just beginning in this most beautiful of Martial Arts. Brazilian Jiu-Jitsu is much more than just an awesome fighting system. It has given colour to my life, seen me through some of the toughest times, and was a much more effective medicine than any prescribed by a doctor. In short, after all the Martial Arts that I had tried, BJJ was the one that fitted me perfectly. I have heard it said that when you find something you love doing, then you will never work a day in your life. BJJ has obviously made me one lazy man because, through all the years in search of perfection, I have never worked one day. It is all play. Which I suppose makes me something of a playboy.

The Hugh Hefner of BJJ. I can live with that.

The Holy Grail

So, there I was, with a black belt in Brazilian Jiu-Jitsu and a lifetime of training, fighting and competing behind me. But what had I really learned on this great voyage of discovery? Well, I theorise that a Martial Artist can be one of two things, a realist or a fantasist. And, regardless of what system you train in, it is how you approach your training that ultimately dictates how efficient its arsenal of techniques will be in a self defence situation. When I first started, on what was to become a lifelong love affair, I was a fantasist. Blindly believing that there are mystical and almost superman-like powers inherent within Martial systems. I wasn't alone. Most of the population growing up in the Bruce Lee boom time that permeated the early 1970's wore rose coloured Kung Fu spectacles. We doggedly refused to question the 'secret' techniques that we saw our celluloid heroes dishing out to the bad guys. In our warped world view, of course the death touch was a bona fide technique, that had probably led to Bruce Lee shuffling off of this mortal coil. We didn't let the truth tame our overactive imaginations. In time, I became a realist. I was forced to be, having been on the receiving end of beatings by multiple opponents, having drag out, knock out brawls against tough, yet untrained people intent on doing me some serious harm. Waking up covered in bruises after trying techniques I didn't know well enough. And, rather than blaming my inadequacy and lack of skill in applying the techniques from whatever system I was studying, I chose to dismiss the art as a whole. I was always searching for the Martial Arts equivalent of the Holy Grail.

If there *was* a Holy Grail in Martial terms, I believe it to be 'Aliveness'. Aliveness is a concept that I was introduced to many years ago, way before I was able to fully understand or grasp its importance. In short, aliveness is pressure-testing techniques against non-compliant opponents - something that is amiss in the majority of traditional systems. Granted, there is sparring in most martial arts and, although this is a form of aliveness, it isn't enough to truly breathe life into your dead patterns and techniques. Not if you want to be able to defend yourself. I believe that, unless you throw out the rule book and fight outside the confines of your chosen art, then all you will ultimately be effective against is someone using the same set of techniques. Someone that moves in the same way and does what is expected, as dictated by the art they are studying. This is why the first Ultimate Fighting Challenge was so important for the development of the martial arts. It dared to pit fighters from diverse arts against each other. However, as the UFC has evolved, rules have been implemented and it is now governed by strict regulations, which have placed it firmly into the sporting arena. MMA vs MMA. Sport and realistic combat should never be mistaken as one and the same thing. Eye gouging, biting, weapons and environment make training for the event of an unprepared attack very hard, if not impossible, to plan for.

Geoff Thompson was amongst the first to pressure-test his Karate skills in his now legendary 'animal days'. The *animal day* concept was to glove up and verbally berate your opponent before launching into a full-on attack. The fight didn't stop if the combatants ended up on the floor, it ended when there was some kind of conclusion, or should that be concussion. It aimed to simulate a real fight as closely as it could. Geoff had realised that without the mental and physical pressures that are common to an unprovoked attack, then preparing for a violent confrontation was nearly an impossible ask. But even these *animal day* training sessions are not 'real attacks'. We will never know how we will respond in a self defence situation until it happens. Adrenal dump can act as a friend or foe when the reality of an attack hits you harder than a good right hook. Fight or flight syndrome is our bodies natural defence system. In other words, you will either choose to stay and fight or run for the hills. Both decisions can save you, depending on the severity of the threat. For example, deciding to stand and fight an attacker armed with a knife could prove fatal, whereas running away could literally save your life. If you can learn to harness the adrenal dump and begin to understand that it can make your reactions quicker and act as a pain nullifier you will better understand the physical body. People have a hard time understanding the reactions of their bodies in times of acute stress. Having worked the doors and dealt with some very threatening behaviours, I learned how to use my body language to psyche out people that were bigger, stronger and younger than me (most of the punters). I realised that the feeling you get in these situations is not fear, it is adrenaline, the brains' superpower. I knew that in all likelihood the would-be attacker was unsure as to the outcome of their actions. I also knew that, in the main, your *average Joe* couldn't tell the effects of adrenaline from fear. They were mainly behaving out of character as a result of drink or drug use. Most could hardly stand up, let alone fight. I was very confident in both my mental strength and my physical skills. As the saying goes, "confidence is king." And this beat more Weekend Warriors than any combative response. I only stopped working the doors recently at 55 years old. I now teach a lot of young door lads, Police Officers and Military personnel how to deal with conflict. And a lot of this training is in line with my theories on aliveness and the importance of understanding the minds' fight or flight receptors.

What *aliveness* and training in such situational scenarios as Geoff Thompsons 'animal days' model does, and does well, is prepare the combatant for non-compliance. The title of this book may at first glance upset die-hard Karate ka. That is not my intention. As they say, *you should never judge a book by its cover*. To the contrary, I know that Karate is a very practical combat system, if trained properly. I have several friends that are more than capable of using Karate in a self defence situation. But, these are Martial Artists that have had some experience of a brutal and unprovoked attack, they have *worked the doors* and have been privy, at first hand, to the dangers that are apparent in an increasingly lawless society. They have adapted their training to make it fit for purpose. Brazilian Jiu-Jitsu is no different. If your reason for training is to defend yourself then you had better be prepared to put yourself into some very uncomfortable situations. Today, most practicing BJJ students focus on the sporting application of BJJ. They pay little time or attention to its' self defence techniques. You need only look at a typical 'randori' or sparring session whereby the 'roll' starts already on the floor and there is no striking allowed. However, by training in an *alive* way, it is probable that your average sport-oriented BJJ student would come out on top in a one on one fight where, after a few punches have been thrown, the fight ends up on the ground (presuming they haven't been knocked out before getting the fight to the ground). I hear deriders of BJJ say time and again, "Well, if you're on the ground with me I can bite and eye gouge." My response is that the BJJ student can also employ these tactics but in a more efficient way due to their ability to control and immobilise their adversary.

In recent years I have become increasingly sceptical of Martial Arts schools who sell themselves as a realistic self defence system. A *one stop shop* that fits all, when clearly these people are often teaching outdated and ridiculous techniques that may well have been effective in feudal Japan when heavy armour slowed things down but, in today's society, these same techniques are about as much use as a chocolate fire guard. It never ceases to dumbfound me when I see knife defences. How many times, apart from in old black and white movies, do you see a would-be knife attacker holding the knife above their head and arching it down towards you? In my experience, most knife attacks are opportunistic, devious and take you by surprise. Rarely, if the attacker intends to stab you, do they a) show you the blade and b) only thrust it once and hold it out for you to use one of the techniques you have perfected in the dojo against your mate Barry who is wielding a rubber practice knife. Try wearing a white t-shirt and get someone to try and mark you with a felt tip pen as you try to disarm them. You will be surprised at the number of marks on your shirt at the end of the exercise. I was lucky in my experience against people carrying blades. In all situations I was shown the blade and had a chance to react or get away. In all probability, the people I was able to defeat had no intention of stabbing me, but you can never be sure. And then there is my absolute all-time favourite, the "No Touch Knockout Masters". What the Hell is that all about? It beggars belief that intelligent people still buy into this bullshit. I often wonder, when watching some 'Master' waving his arms about and dropping his student with his powerful 'Chi', whether it is really a bad case of halitosis that takes their legs from under them. But, no matter how many times these 'Masters' are KO'd by a non-believer, their schools keep flourishing. If any No Touch Masters want to come to my gym and prove me wrong, please do. The problem with people wanting to learn a martial art as a self defence system is that their research is based on TV and the Movie industry which still propagate the myths that have been around for many years. Like I have stressed, in my opinion, there are no bad Martial Arts (apart from those No Touch systems) only bad practitioners. So, depending on what art you choose, it makes sense to check out the instructors' credentials. After all, would you feel confident being taught to swim by someone that has never been in the water? Sounds ludicrous, but there are many, and I mean many, Martial arts 'experts' (that are making a very decent living) that have never been in a fight, teaching people that have also never been in a fight, how to fight. I'm not advocating going out looking for a fight just to prove yourself. What I do advocate is, *don't wear blinkers*. Question whether something in your system is effective. Usually, a good rule of thumb is in a techniques ease of application. For example, a pre-emptive strike doesn't need to look good to work. A solid hook or cross from Western or Thai boxing or a good reverse punch from Karate, if practiced enough, will do what it says on the tin. Learn how to fight in all ranges. It is not enough to say, "Well my techniques are so good that no one would get me on the ground, so I don't need to learn that Jiu-Jitsu stuff." Shit happens. You could be fighting on an icy pavement, or you could be dragged to the floor from behind before you have had a chance to apply your stand up skills.

Same with those people that only concentrate their training on the ground. The Gracie family famously said, "95% of fights end up on the floor." Whilst this may be true, a higher percentage start on the feet. Do you know how to get the fight to the ground, if that is your preferred arena? Judo and wrestling are great arts to supplement BJJ and vice versa. For me, the best piece of advice on self defence came from my Dad when he said, "Hit first, hit hard and don't stop until the fight is over." These 'street fighters' that often contact me to say that they think they would make great MMA fighters, are talking about two completely different things. Your average street fighter, if such a beast exists, is probably well schooled in the art of the sniper attack. That being an offensive that isn't announced. This is different to a 'straightener' whereby the two combatants are prepared for a fight. The sniper often launches his or her attack from angles that are hard to defend i.e. from behind, the side, or when the target is in a compromised position, such as sitting or laying down. In my opinion, this sort of 'street fighter' is a coward, they often don't have the minerals for a fair fight. This type of fighter wouldn't get into a ring or a cage to compete against an equally skilled opponent. The pre-emptive strike is different. It is utilised when an aggressor is upping their level of threat. A good pre-emptive strike is the best course of action in this scenario, as being on the receiving end of the first strike can often be hard to recover from, although not impossible.

For all around good self defence an awareness of environment is essential. A self defence course that starts with physical techniques such as kicking and punching is, in my view, a waste of time. Self defence doesn't have to be about fighting. It should be about awareness, avoidance and common sense approaches. Bruce Lee talked about *the art of fighting without fighting*. Only sometimes we are left with little choice but to defend ourselves physically. And this is where practical techniques will serve you the best. Again, Bruce Lee said, "Adapt what is useful and discard the rest." In other words, keep the flowery, crowd-pleasing stuff for the dojo. It has its place, but its place is not outside the kebab shop at 2.00am on a Friday night when some neanderthal is poking you in the chest.

Having espoused all that, my two penneth worth if you like, (what do I know) I am still a fan of all of the Martial arts, regardless of what style, where it comes from or what it claims to do (apart from that no touch knockout stuff). I believe that the benefits it gives such as health and wellbeing, fitness, discipline and respect are priceless. I value the Black belts I hold in different martial arts. To gain a black belt shows tenacity, commitment and loyalty. Traits that are often lacking in some areas of this modern world we live in. I love to see anyone that is exceptional in what they do, be it Kata or points fighting, MMA or Jiu-Jitsu. I still get the same buzz watching Bruce Lee in 'The Way of The Dragon' beating up a very hairy Chuck Norris, or latterly Jackie Chan and Tony Jaa. I consider myself a Martial Artist first and foremost. It has been my lifetimes' passion. And the flame still burns as brightly today as it did way back when, witnessing the incredible Steve Cattle's snap that he got at the end of his reverse punch, or the first time I caught an arm bar in rolling.

37

Don't Believe the Hype

"Fame is the thirst of youth." Lord Byron

In 2017 I received a letter saying that I was being inducted into the UK Martial Arts Hall of Fame.

I had trained for the best part of 40 years in various combat systems, but it was Brazilian Jiu-Jitsu that really held my heart in its hands. I had spent a lifetime developing my skills, both on tarmac and tatami and I had taught many people over the years both the self defence and the sporting applications of Martial Arts. I certainly didn't consider myself *famous*. What is fame any way, but an ego-induced title? But, I was proud of my achievements and the award was a way of celebrating the time and effort I had put in. Plus, it would be something to tell the Grandkids one day.

The award was to be presented by American superstar, Bill 'Superfoot' Wallace, a living legend that went way back to those halcyon days before we became obsessed with MMA. I was dressed in a new suit and, if I say so myself, I looked okay for someone on the wrong side of 50. As my name was called, I asked my friend to get a good photo and I set off on the long walk to collect my certificate. 'Superfoot' proffered his hand as he handed me the certificate and, looking at me up and down said, "You're wearing your tie clip too high."

Now, I know that I should have smiled, taken my certificate and walked, but it didn't go down like that. It must have been the old Mod in me that decided to come out and play as I looked Superfoot squarely in the eye and replied, "You're an American, what do you know of style?"

I caught the old legend off guard with my comeback and, although he offered a weak smile, I could tell he wasn't overly impressed. What the hell, I was officially famous - I could say what I wanted. But seriously, it was a great night and a true honour to be inducted into the UK Martial Arts Hall of Fame. Though, as I was to discover, no accolade or award could shield you from those things that lay hidden in plain sight.

And if we don't know what we are fighting, we are always going to be caught off guard.

38

My Ever-Changing Moods

"You just can't beat the person who won't give up." Babe Ruth

From my earliest recollection I have always felt somewhat lost, as if the world is turning and I am out of sync. A song is playing and all around are dancing, but I am frozen, rooted to the spot.

I have days when I am on top of the world. And days that see me staring into an endless blackness; an abyss. Everyone is like this to some degree. We all have ups and downs, at least I think we do. The rollercoaster of emotions that separate us from the animals and mammals with whom we share this spinning ball we call Earth. Only, for some, the despair, the loneliness and the utter helplessness are more than just a fleeting change in mood that is dictated by the ticking of the clock, the changing of the season, or the words used as a weapon from another. For some, the ever-changing mood is a result of a more complex issue.

It had been a rollercoaster of a ride. A lifetime stretched behind me like a road map showing all the wrong turns I had been down. With age comes wisdom, or rather, that should be the case. I think I missed out on the wisdom part, but I hadn't dodged the age bullet. I had lived the life of a fighter. The scars running deep, a lasting testament to the battles fought. Each etched into the skin by blade, knuckle, or whatever creative way that one human being can use to disfigure another, whether through the act of hatred, aggression or sporting endeavor.

The only scars that aren't so apparent are those we carry beneath the skin. The battles that have resulted in these invisible scars are often the most bloody and barbaric of all encounters. They come from facing a demon or, in some cases, an army of demons. A devastating and relentless force. The demon's weapons, depression, anxiety and self-loathing, take a hold of you at the most vulnerable times of your life. You have as much control over these emotions as a paper bag that is caught in a twister. Flailing about, unable to find rest or peace, when and where it will end, if it does, is an unknown. You have little choice but to ride it out and hope for the best.

Sometimes, the outwardly confident and carefree are carrying the heaviest of chains around, like the Dickensian tale of Marley's ghost. It is only when we accept that we are in this inner battle that we can prepare. My battles had appeared to always be fought with clenched fist and backed up by my Jiu-Jitsu skills, at least, that's what I wanted people to think. Happy-go-lucky old me.

But, out of view and on the inside, there raged a war. The real danger comes when you are backed into a corner, feeling helpless and unprepared. If this happens you might as well pull out a chair and watch your whole life from relationship breakdown to addiction, unfold like a bad B-movie, forcing you to live your own version of Groundhog Day. And worse, we can pass our demons onto our children, like a bad debt that never quite gets repaid, surely the worst kind of inheritance.

Of all the battles I have been in, I am proudest of my small victories to banish the inner demon. Self-destruction was always my masterpiece, my *special curse*. It made me run into battles I knew I couldn't win. It made me destroy things that matter above all others, and it made me get up time and again and say, "Let's go again."

Courage comes in the darkest of hours, when all hope seems lost and you feel truly alone. I was about to face my blackest hour, and I had no clue how I would fare, or even if I would survive.

The only certainty was that I was about to come face to face with my demon, my ultimate opponent.

39

Get Up, Stand Up

"Never confuse a single defeat with a final defeat."
F. Scott Fitzgerald

The cold steel of the knife pressed into my neck. My left hand tightened the grip I had on the bottle of pills. The room seemed to close in. I struggled to breathe. My eyes locked onto the blue spinning light that illuminated a darker than normal autumnal evening sky. Inside was the strangest mix of calm and energy. Outside, panic, as people tried to make themselves heard and seen. But the only voices I could hear came from deep inside my head. There seemed to be an argument raging, as one voice said, "Do it," and the other asked, "Why?"

I was at a crossroads. Before me stood the Devil, waiting patiently for his pound of flesh, behind me the road much-travelled. I had faced this demon many times, and many times I had fallen.

That night had been the darkest I can recall. I had been low before, but this time I had decided that enough was enough. I had my back against a cold wall. Nowhere to go. No options left. It was just a toss-up between opening the veins and letting the blood run freely away, or to take the pills and drift off. Strangely, I felt calm, as if this was the most natural thing in the world. I had no fear, just a sense of acceptance. The book of my life had reached its final chapter. I was sick and tired of being sick and tired. At 54 years old, I was bloody ancient, an embarrassment to the still 18-year-old Mod that lived and raged beneath the wrinkles and greying hair. I sent a text to my family and a few close friends, "Sorry". No more words needed.

The police and ambulance came soon after. My fall from grace not such a secret affair, after all. I hadn't seen a change, but apparently it was as clear as the brightest of days. My behaviour had become increasingly bizarre. Conversations I had had with family and friends in the days leading up to 'the breakdown' were analysed and debated. The text, giving validation that I had 'lost it', whatever 'it' was. I was taken to hospital and steps were taken to safeguard me.

A series of interviews with the Psychiatric team followed. My past came flooding out, as if a can of Coke had been shaken vigorously before being opened. Notebooks were scribbled on, nods and sympathetic smiles offered, as the professionals made their appraisal.

I was referred to a Psychiatrist, my story to be re-told, a diagnosis to be made.

40

Shine On You Crazy Diamond.

Mad Hatter: "Have I gone mad?"
Alice: "I'm afraid so. You're entirely bonkers. But I'll tell you a secret. All the best people are." Lewis Carroll

I had some knowledge of Bipolar Disorder, but I had never really taken the time to really understand it. At least, until I was told that I was Bipolar.

An important part of any fight is knowing your opponent. What are their strengths and weaknesses? The more you know about what, or who, you are fighting, the better chance you have of coming out on top. Here is my fight research.

Bipolar Disorder or, as it was previously known, Manic Depression, is a mental illness that can lead to periods of intense highs and equally intense low mood orientation. During the highs, there is a feeling that you can do anything, achieve goals that were previously considered out of reach (e.g. write a book and have it published). Behaviours, during this phase, can vary but making rash and unwise decisions that can lead to personal harm or risk are not uncommon. The 'high' is seen as a very creative phase with long periods of activity and little sleep being needed (most of this book was written in this phase, as you can probably tell). It is not uncommon for paranoia and hallucinations during this stage. I was convinced a few years ago, after a particularly intense high, when I had been awake for 3 days straight, that I was being followed by 70's singer Lionel Ritchie, and worse he was able to shape-shift and take the form of a chair (I wouldn't mind but I hate his songs; Paul Weller I could have handled). Sounds ludicrous as I write this, but to me, it was very real. The lows are, as the name implies, the polar-opposite, whereby a feeling of helplessness and self-depreciation are often apparent. Suicidal thoughts are not uncommon during this phase. The shift in moods makes for an unpredictable life. Addictions, such as drugs, alcohol and gambling often go hand in hand with Bipolar and these addictions are a form of self-medicating. However, trying to treat Bipolar in this way is usually when things break down and the spiral is hard to understand or deal with. It is usually at this point (if you are lucky) that a professional intervention and diagnosis are made and subsequently treated, as it was in my case.

Apparently, I had had this illness, or at least a form of it, all my life. It may explain the rages, the bouts of depression and mania, and the rash and often wrong decisions I had made along the way.

For me, my childhood is a time that I struggle to comprehend. It is as if I am looking back on a life that wasn't mine, something I never really owned. I often ask my brother what my childhood was like and he is mostly able to fill in the blanks, although he only saw the person I allowed him and others to see. I am able to recall the significant events, but can't seem to piece together the jigsaw that made me a whole person. It's as if some of the pieces are missing, or stolen. Later, in my teenage years, I desperately wanted to fit in. But, because I wasn't like people in my peer group, I had to create a way of being accepted. My inability to feel comfortable in social situations often led to frustration and violence, which gave birth to a kind of self-fulfilling prophecy. In other words, I lost any identity I had, and played the role I thought was mine within the group. In adulthood, I found relationships difficult. They all started well. I can be quite the charmer, and if I'm in the mood, fun to be around (honestly). But the problem was that there was always this other me trying to break out. This 'other me' manifested as cold and distant. I was capable of shutting out the very people that loved me. My addictive gene saw me either partying too hard or training all the time, rarely giving time to my partner. And when I wasn't training I was bouncing between *Mr Happy* and *Mr The End of the World is Nigh*, like the metal ball in a never-ending game of pinball. People told me that my 'problem' was depression. But that was never the right diagnosis. I wasn't sad, or down in the dumps all of the time, I didn't feel lost or alone. Only sometimes. I just felt different, a one of a kind. Only that wasn't true. There are many like me apparently. Others that are square pegs trying to fit into round holes. It sometimes feels like I'm an alien, merely visiting a new orbit before I am breaking the speed of light back to planet 'fucked up'. And yet, much like a functioning alcoholic, I seem to get by. And, like the functioning alcoholic, I am good at covering my tracks. Painting on a smile, cracking a joke, masking the real mood. I blag with the skill of a Shakespearean actor. I can even tie my own shoelaces and have had enough resolve to try to make something of myself. I have a career. I have ambition, drive and determination and a laser-like vision when something fires my imagination. Whilst at other times I just drift along, going with the tide, not caring where I end up. Doing the bare minimum to survive. I know, for example, that I need to eat and drink in order to survive, but there is no passion attached to any endeavour and, at these times, I let myself go. Uncaring as to what people think of me. It is a constant battle between the two polar extremes. An unknown as to which is the stronger on any given day. I imagine that there is a need for some light and shade in everyone's life. If I was always 'up' there is the chance of burn out, and if I was always 'down', well, there is only so far you can go.

Anyway, I rallied against the label but, in the end, like a well sunk-in choke, I had to admit defeat and tap-out. At least, until I found a way out of the hold that it had on me.

I was prescribed strong medication. So strong, that I was unable to function. The dosage made me groggy, unsteady and blunt in every sense of the word. I tried the tablets, I wanted to give it a chance, and besides, the alternative might be a lot worse.

As the days melted into each other and I slept for hours on end, no interest in anything or anyone, I started to resent this legal drugging. What kind of a life was it when you can't function, hold a conversation or be creative? In truth, I missed the highs. During these spikes in energy I felt untouchable, able to do anything, unstoppable. Now, I was a hollow representation of the man I had been. There had to be a way of leading a life that still offered excitement and opportunity, where I could be the happy, energised me, without the *dark side* casting its long shadow. I liked Mr Hyde. Dr Jekyll was a tad boring.

But, I was a long way from finding the answers to the questions that crept into my mind. If I was to compare this struggle to a fight, then I was being hit from every possible angle, losing every round, and seconds away from my corner throwing in the towel. But, like all the great fights throughout history, the ones in which the underdog comes good in the end, just maybe I could cause the upset, turn the tide in my favour and pull off a Rocky Balboa moment.

I knew that I wasn't going to change things by sitting back and accepting my fate. I decided that I needed to take back some control. Although stopping the mania, the dosage I was prescribed was also stopping me living my life the way I wanted.

I had an appointment booked to see my Psychiatrist. This was my time to tell him that I needed to stop the medication or, at least, if not stop altogether, then get the dosage reduced to a level that didn't make me feel like a zombie. The Psychiatrist didn't agree to me stopping the medication altogether, but he did agree to a reduction, with a further reduction in a few months if my condition remained stable. It was a start.

I battled everyday just to lift my head off the pillow, fighting the demon constantly, sometimes feeling that I was faring well, and at other times I took a bloody and humiliating beating at his hands.

I had to force myself to leave the house. Some days, the curtains remained closed, my phone switched off. I started to believe that I was being followed. That someone was watching me. I would pace the floor, telling myself that it was all in my mind, but I doubted my own sanity and believed the worst. If I was at the gym, I found it hard to keep up an act. People started noticing I was different, although no one told me that they were concerned.

I suppose mental health is an illness that is more than capable of hiding in plain sight. I was doing my best to fool some of the people some of the time, but as the saying goes, *you can't fool all the people all the time*. My family kept a close eye on me too, but I was lying to them so that they would feel better and not worry. I had been a chameleon most of my life, so convincing people that I was doing okay, wasn't too much of a stretch.

But the person that I was lying to most was me. I knew that I was far from being emotionally and mentally well. What really scared me was the fact that I had been ill all my life and hadn't known. There were times in my childhood, and later, that were an absolute give away, but I had failed to see them. And, in all honesty, writing this book has really helped me to step outside of the story and see how screwed up I was. But even though I now had some insight into my condition, I still had no clue how I was going to beat it or, more to the point, if I could beat it. I had met people that were on medication and accepting of the fact that this was their life now, but they weren't fighters, and I was. There was a difference. I knew that I had to keep moving forward, one step at a time. Inch by inch, second by second and day by day.

The problem with using medication to treat my condition was that I had lost control of the situation. That was something difficult to accept. I was unable to make any real headway because, in truth, I was inside a bubble. A bubble that I had to burst out of before I could even see the enemy. Prior to my diagnosis, I had self-medicated with alcohol. Even the Martial Arts, my raison d'etre, were a form of therapy, and thank God I had the training because, in all honesty, I'm not sure where I would be today. I came to realise that what I had done all my life to get through these episodes wasn't working anymore. Maybe the training, competing and having the goal of being a BJJ Black Belt had helped me dodge a few bullets but, in the end, it wasn't enough to stop the Demon completely. I needed something more than physical preparation.

When you are desperate, confused and frightened, these are the things that make you fight with all your heart and soul. You must. The alternative is unacceptable. It had been 6 months since my nightmare had begun. I can't, in all honesty, tell you what was going on each and every day, but I know that I was still in the fight. Just.

There was one thing for sure - I wasn't about to roll over and give in. That was something I knew with certainty. I had been fighting since the day the Dr had pulled me kicking and screaming into this world. Since that day, I've been slashed with blade, glassed, punched, kicked and stomped on. My jaw has been broken, as have my ribs, fingers and toes, not to mention my heart. What passes for my left ear resembles a half-chewed Quaver crisp. I'm held together by stitch and glue like a latter day Frankenstein's Monster, and if I don't wake each morning with some degree of pain, I've obviously died in my sleep. But one thing I don't do is give up without a fight.

I came to realise that I had been preparing for this opponent all my life. Everything that had happened, each blow that had knocked me down had shaped me, made me strong, made me get up time and again. Each hardship endured was really a life lesson from which I had to grow, even those that were impossible to accept at the time like the senseless death of my daughters. I had been close to death, and I had seen death; not only seen it but looked it squarely in the eye. Martial Arts had been the forge that sharpened my sword. But, more than the physical aspects, I had taken much from the philosophies that run through the core of the fighting arts. If my mind wasn't working properly and these mood swings were my Kryptonite, then I had to develop a defence and a suitable offence that would help me to survive. If my past had taught me anything it was to never take your opponent lightly, that fair play was for those that deserved it, and actions speak louder than words. This fucker was about to get a can of Whoop Ass opened on it because if ever there was a time to come out fighting, then this was it. I had been getting the proverbial shit kicked out of me for two years now.

41

Losing My Religion

"Religion. It's given people hope in a world torn apart by religion."
Jon Stewart

I was never a religious man, but I did, and do, believe that there is something that is greater than humankind. A *higher presence*.

Some call it God, although it goes by many names. Others believe that the universe will provide, and that all you must do is ask. I was somewhere in the middle. I was never going to be one of those Sunday morning *'all things bright and beautiful'* Bible-bashers or, for that matter, a tree-hugging Hippy, but I did place some stock in a belief that there is more than just the here and now. That all things, good or bad, are lessons from which we grow as human beings. I had nothing to lose in asking whatever this *greater thing* was.

Now, talking to yourself is considered a form of madness, but address your questions to this invisible force (God, Allah, Buddha) and it's perfectly acceptable. The problem arises when you believe you have seen these religious figureheads or, worse, that they talk back to you. If that happens, the first to condemn you are the very same people that turn up every Sunday to worship, praise and talk about the Second Coming. You, on the other hand, are likely going to end up in a place that has nice padded walls, and I don't mean a Jiu-Jitsu or MMA gym. Madness is a matter of perspective obviously. Anyhow, I was talking to whatever and whoever was listening in. I asked many questions, but I'm disappointed to say that I never got a visit from God, his Son, The Holy Ghost, or the Easter Bunny, for that matter. At least, I don't think I did. That's not to say that I wasn't given an answer. I believe that I was. But it came from a place and time long gone. You might say, I was shown not only the light at the end of the tunnel, but I had one foot in the sunshine.

42

A Change is Gonna Come

"If you can quit for a day, you can quit for a lifetime." Benjamin Alire Saenz

I debated calling this chapter 'The Drugs Don't Work', the only song I really like or, for that matter know, by The Verve but felt it too cliched given the subject matter. Instead, it was Sam Cooke's masterpiece, "A Change is Gonna Come" that acted as my muse and gave inspiration to write this part of the narrative. The lyric is delivered with so much passion and raw emotion that it is hard not to be moved. It's as if the song is reaching into you, touching your very soul. Cooke sings about a fight for freedom in a time that was both oppressive and dangerous during the early days of the Civil Rights Movement. But it could be about any struggle. There is a real hope and positivity in this beautiful song that seems as relevant today as it did in 1964, when Cooke wrote it. The line, 'It's been too hard living, but I'm afraid to die,' resonated with me. And, for me, a change was definitely gonna come, but only if I took control and got off of the medication that had held me prisoner for the past two years.

At the point of being prescribed the drug, I was in a state of not knowing whether I was coming or going. A Psychiatrist told me that the drug would give me some equilibrium. I was so out of it I had taken my friend with me to relay the information later to me. The 'wonder drug' was Quietapine. I was given a choice of several drugs that would fare equally well in the battle against Dr Evil Bipolar. In truth, I agreed to Quietapine after one of the side effects by another leading brand was the possibility of your hair falling out and growing back curly. This shows where my cognitive functioning was. I was making decisions based on my bloody hair do. I gave little thought to the other possible side effects, the most common being, chills, cold sweats, confusion, dizziness, sleepiness or drowsiness, weight gain, constipation, increased serum cholesterol, sedated state, loss of balance and painful or difficult urination. And that list is without the real risk to liver function. What's not to love? And I went along with it because, like many of us, a white coat means absolute understanding and power. Whilst the drug initially stopped the suicidal thoughts and mania, it also stopped every other emotion. I was incapable of doing anything.

The drug had stolen the most human gift we possess, the ability to feel. Whether the feeling is good or bad is irrelevant. We need to feel. It is what separates us from the other tenants on this beautiful blue ball.

It took me two long years of *just being* to realise that this is not a quality of life. At this point, I will say that medication does work for some, it's just that, for me, it didn't. I had the odd glimpse through the Quietapine haze of the 'old me'. But they were few and far between. In the main, I had become a hologram, all body and no soul. I was coasting through life, but that only became possible as the medication, at my insistence, was reduced. Initially I was prescribed such a high dose, that I lived in fear of falling and hitting my head at home, dying alone. This sounds dramatic, but anyone that has ever been on these drugs will tell you that they hit you harder than Mike Tyson. I was unable to drive, work or train. I spent my days drooling on the sofa and my nights desperately trying to get to my bed without falling. My weight ballooned. I was living in a state of almost dream-like serenity but was in fact a living, breathing nightmare.

This was just another part of the battle but it was integral to me getting my life back. I realised that I had to not only reduce the drugs, but to get off them completely. Now, this sounds simplistic and, in an ideal world, it might have been easier than it has proven to be. Stopping taking this kind of medication, without due care and advice, can be at the worst fatal and at the best very risky (take medical advice before trying this). Every time I saw my Psychiatrist, I told him that the level of dosage was wrong and that I needed to come off the drug. He would listen in that way that Psychiatrists often listen, with one ear tuned to me and the other tuned to his inner voice. The one that told him that 'most' bipolar sufferers, at some point, will decide that they are 'well again', and therefore thanks, but no thanks to the handsomely packaged miracle pill that could cure all of our 'issues'.

I was strong with him and insistent that he should at least help me work towards getting off the pills in the future. He agreed to small reductions in the dosage which, over time, got me back to work, driving and training. But it never gave me the one thing I craved, *my sense of self*, back. During what was to be my final 'consultation', but which was actually more a verbal sparring match, he decided that rather than reduce the dosage, he would arrange for a slower release version of the all-singing, all-dancing 'Soul Shrinker'. He told me, "You will be on medication for the rest of your life." In other words, 'accept your fate'. The old me, if ever there was such a person, was dead and gone. In his place, an intruder. A bit like that version of Spiderman that wore the black latex outfit and decided that he was 'the new and improved' not-so-friendly neighbourhood Spiderman. Only, I wasn't left with all the skills Bad Spidey had. I was to resign myself to a life of blending in. Of losing my way. Just another lemming headed for the edge of the cliff, following in stooped silence as, one after another, without question, we step off and fall to the rocks below.

I said earlier that the pills stopped the mania and lows. That wasn't always true, I was still having a watered-down version of both. At times animated enough to fool people that my 'spark' had returned and at other times so low that I could look at a light fitting wondering if it would hold my weight. I didn't really want to die, I wanted to live. But not the way I was, through the banality that comes from a drug induced state. I knew, and know, that I could never end my life in such a way that would damage my kids, the people that love me and my friends, but I also felt hopeless.

Shortly after 'the final consultation', I hit a low that had me taking to my bed. Sobbing for no reason (although I have always been weepy at sad films), losing all hope of a 'fairytale happy ending' and generally giving up trying. I went to the pill box like it was calling me through a Pied Piper-like call to arms. Took the 'magic formula' and waited until I was so drowsy I didn't care anymore. This had been my life for two years. I went off sick again, unable to work. I stopped teaching Jiu-Jitsu. I stopped doing anything but popping pills and eating. My friend insisted that I see the psychiatrist. It was not only a good plan, it was the only plan I had. I got myself hyped up for another round with the shrink. He was a good man, his heart was in the right place, he just didn't have enough resolve to question the practice of medicine that has been handed down throughout the ages. And that's fine. There needs to be people in white coats. Experts in their field, be it a Dr of medicine or the mind, they do an amazing job. But I believe that there are other answers to psychiatric problems, and I wanted to look at these and get away from the road much travelled.

A telephone call to book an appointment led not only to surprise, but utter shock when I was told by the receptionist that I had been discharged from the care of the Mental Health team. What about my medication, my ongoing battle to get off the drug? Not only that, but the Psychiatrist had told me that he was going to recommend a 'slow release' version. None of this had been done. I had, in effect, been 'kicked to the curb'. I hadn't even had a letter telling me of the intention to discharge me. I felt both let down, but also liberated. This was a sign that if I was to get off the meds, then this was my time to put up or shut up. To either take back control or accept my lot.

I saw my GP. I asked how I should go about 'cold turkey', coming off the drug that had been my jailer for the best part of two years. I told him that I had already started cutting the pills in two, thus halving the dosage. He said that this was not the best course of action and re-refferred me to the Mental Health team. I told him that this had proven fruitless in the past and that it was my intention to help myself.

Day One. Or One Day

So, with a goal in mind, I set out to free myself from the latest in a long line of addictions that have gripped me over the years. Some habits are easier to break than others. I was now 5 months alcohol free. I hadn't eaten meat for over two years and felt better for both abstains. But these pills were a different matter. Unbeknown to me, they had taken a hold of me in a way that would be difficult to escape from. But, fear is a strong motivator in any battle, and these tablets, as innocent as they looked, were just the opposite. I knew that I couldn't just stop overnight. The 'Cold Turkey' approach wouldn't cut it here. I had started to diminish the dosage myself, cutting the pills in half. But my morning after taking the drug was still a hazy brain fog reality. After three weeks of my best efforts to reduce the dosage, the time came for me to try and go a night without the pill. And what a long night that turned out to be. Rip Van Winkle was nowhere to be found, and I tossed and turned all night long (Don't worry, I'm not having another Lionel Ritchie moment). As I paced the floor, talking to myself and generally getting into a hyped-up state, I realised that this was perhaps the greatest benefit of the tablets - they stilled my mind. I have always found it hard to quiet the internal voices in my head. I justify this by believing that my best ideas come to me in the dead of night, when there is no distraction. But we all need sleep. There is only so long you can go without it. But, as long and restless as that first day and night had been, I felt something different as the sun broke through the endless darkness. Gone was the cloudy mind that I had become so used to that I took it as the norm. I felt so alive. Creative. Free. I went the whole day and night in a state of hyper energy. One of my Jiu-Jitsu students, Hazel, has come to know my mood swings really well, and that night at Jiu-Jitsu, as I bounced around the mat like a demented Tigger, she fixed me with her Ninja-like stare and said, "Oh God." We both laughed, but she later told me that she sometimes dreaded these 'highs' because the 'low' was never too far behind, like an ever-present shadow that was getting bigger by the day. That night, at bedtime, I was still as lit up as Blackpool sea front. The lights were on, but there was definitely no one home. It got to 3.00am and still no respite. I tried everything from counting sheep to trying self-hypnosis. Nothing worked. I was trapped on a hamster wheel that I couldn't get off. In desperation I took a pill, and within half an hour my mind had stilled and I was in the land of nod. I woke feeling drunk. A horrible thought hit me. *If I couldn't sleep without these pills, I was screwed.*

I felt like a failure. I had succumbed to the pills. I knew I had to take a tactical retreat, but on the next offensive I was determined to stay off the pills, even if it meant two or more days without sleep. I wanted to be so exhausted that by 9.00pm I would be unable to stay awake. I trained hard that night in class, rolling with all my students until my Gi was soaked and heavy with my sweat. My body knew it had been in a war, but my mind was still razor-sharp. I knew that this was another 24 hours of watching the dark night sky as it faded to morning blue. Another battle to contain the chimp-like chatter of my agitated mind. It is hard to describe this feeling, but it is like your mind is a busy train station. The trains come from all directions, carrying passengers, rushing to their destinations, without care of trampling over others in their quest to be first. Only, they are not people, they are thoughts. Each vying to be heard and seen. My brain would ache in this chaotic and surreal existence. The pain was unbearable but I had to get past this. I knew that this was the hardest part. Sleep deprivation is a powerful thing, which is why it is used as a means of torture. I was certainly being tortured and ready to crack under the pressure. But one thing kept coming back to me. A thought so loud that it drowned out the combined chatter of all the other passengers that night. *If I could achieve a Black Belt in Brazilian Jiu-Jitsu, I could achieve anything.* I had to do as I had done all those years ago - keep going, even when it felt like a hopeless dream. But I had done it, so this little matter of sleep was not going to railroad my recovery.

It was 48 hours in. Something felt different. I was tired. Not just tired but exhausted. Sleep came that night, and in the morning I awoke feeling like a major part of the battle had been won. It felt amazing. Like that feeling you get when your name is called out and your instructor ties the Blue belt around your waist. You know there is still a long way to go, but you have passed the first milestone on your journey. From here on in, I knew I could beat this. I just had to get through the Purple, Brown and Black belt of *mind Jiu-Jitsu*.

43

Karate Doesn't Work in a Phone Box

"You must be shapeless, formless, like water. When you pour water in a cup, it becomes the cup. When you pour water in a bottle, it becomes the bottle. When you pour water in a teapot, it becomes the teapot. Water can drip and it can crash. Become like water my friend." Bruce Lee

Karate doesn't work in a phone box. How can it? By its very nature, it is a Martial Art that, on the surface, relies on distance. My Dad had said, "Those flowery moves are all well and good, but in a confined space they are no use."

You can't punch or kick in a phone box, so what is the alternative? We must adapt. To use whatever we can, especially if it is our foe who chooses the time, the place, and the battlefield. What, I hear you asking, has a fight in a prehistoric phone box got to do with beating a mental illness? My answer?

Everything.

I realised that I had been fighting this inner demon in a metaphorical phone box, and worse, trying to defeat it with a roundhouse kick or a reverse punch, when I should be using a choke. In a war that was becoming bloodier and more barbaric each day, I was armed with the wrong ammunition. The bullets I used gave the demon strength. I needed a super bullet, like the silver ones that slay the werewolf.

I started to look at alternative ways to bring balance and clarity back into my life. Pills had been a part of the recovery process, but all they really do is take the edge off. I had managed to wean myself off the prescription drugs and was feeling like my strength was building. The haze was gone, and I felt like I could see clearly but I knew that I had to look inward. I needed to accept, much like an alcoholic accepts their addiction, that I had a problem, and that the demon wasn't a separate entity, it was really me. Or, at least a part of me. We weren't different beings. We breathed the same air, looked alike and spoke with the same accent. The only difference being the behaviours that we participated in. I started to realise that the more I fed the demonic me, the more the real me grew weaker. I had to make strong the spirit and stay away from the toxins that were threatening to poison my soul.

But first, all the years of adding layers to conceal the real person had to be stripped back, much like an artist chisels away the stone to reveal the true beauty of the sculpture. I realised that it is beneath the surface that truth lies. The problem in trying to find the *real self* is that we play different roles depending on who or where we are at any given time. For example, we are different in the company of our friends than we are in the company of our work mates. We adapt our personalities in order to fit in. And we do this so many times that our authentic self is buried beneath so many layers that it can suffocate and die under the weight. I had been doing this 'adding of layers' so long that I had no clue as to who the real me was. Was I the violent angry young man that had got into trouble with the police, or the scared and confused child that preferred to hide away most of the time? Or, maybe I was the single-minded man that had chased his dream so long that at the moment he had achieved it, felt like there was nowhere else to go, no reason to go on? Some of these layers had purpose. They had allowed me to survive at different times in my life. But sometimes it is the layers that are added by others that can be the hardest to shed. Childhood is a particularly vulnerable time. We are told who we are and how we should behave. Our young minds are processing thousands of thoughts and influences every day. We are trying to find our place within family and social structures. Growing into our personalities. These layers often don't mature at the same rate as our physical growth. We can hold onto child-like emotions, fears and coping strategies well into adulthood.

All of these layers, whether self-imposed in adulthood or gifted in childhood, play out like a never-ending game of hide and seek, only most of us never get to find the real self. It is only when you see this that we can choose to remove some of the layers and get close to our authentic self. This is never an easy task and is not something that can happen overnight, it is a day to day struggle. The behavioural traits that come with the layers are deeply entrenched and, as such, hard to change. It wasn't going to be easy, but the fact that I understood that there was a need to strip away some of the layers altogether, whilst harnessing others so that I could have a degree of control, gave me a starting point.

The first day that I realised that I had found the answer, I felt liberated. Not only had I stepped into the light, but the shadows that cast behind me were less dark and foreboding. I set about putting together a plan. A way of making myself stronger, in mind body and spirit. My days changed from mind- numbing solitude to stepping out of my front door. I took long walks with my faithful companion Teddy (the King of Dogs). Not only was I walking, but I was connecting with nature. It was as if the blinkers I had worn for many years were removed. As if I could see clearly for the first time in my life. The trees were a beautiful green and brown, the water a deep blue like the pastel colours found in a Van Gogh painting. All around I felt hope, where before there had been none.

I changed my diet, becoming a pescatarian. I stopped drinking. I even took up the guitar again after a long hiatus and bought a new Vespa scooter (once a Mod, always a Mod). And, of course, Jiu-Jitsu, my saviour for many years, was practised with a renewed vigour.

But the main thing that changed was the view I had of my life. It was as if I was back standing on the mountain top in Rio with Christ the Redeemer overlooking the good and bad of the city that stretched below. Only, instead of the Brazilian City with all of its beauty and ugliness, I saw my life. I felt that I had got some control. My moods, although still fluctuating, where more stable. The black days lifted and were replaced by a new optimism. I started to feel happy with myself, something I had struggled with throughout my life. My relationships with family and friends improved. Whereas before I bottled up my emotions, I started to talk about the things that were bothering me. This gave me a release, a valve that could let out the steam gradually, rather than the explosion of anger and frustration. And, at last, I felt like I was finding the real me. I might not be at the point where I am garroting this illness in the phone box, but I am definitely in the fight and, more to the point, I have a winning strategy.

44

The Dream

"Karate Doesn't work in a phone box." Bill Savage

I am standing at a crossroads.

I look ahead, the road stretched before me, empty. On the horizon, a golden sun illuminating all that it touches. I stop, the road to the left and the right clear, inviting, almost beguiling. A cool breeze tickles the hairs on the nape of my neck and I turn to look over my shoulder. The road travelled, showing the many wrong turns and scars that have blighted my journey thus far.

In the distance I see an old-fashioned red phone box. A boy presses his face against the windowpanes, the door opens, and a man steps out. He takes the child's hand and, as they turn to walk away, he stops, raises his hand and waves. I watch mesmerized as the man starts to playfully fight with the child, throwing a slap that is parried. The boy's kick, thrown in retaliation, is easily blocked. The man turns the child's wrist effortlessly, throwing him to the floor, his carpet-slippered foot resting on the boy's neck. He holds the lock until the boy signals surrender. He looks at me again, this time a smile flickers across his face. I raise my hand and acknowledge the scene. I feel a warm glow, through my wrist and into my hand. And, when I look back again, the road, once littered with the mistakes of a past life, is empty.

I keep my face towards the sun. I don't need to look behind anymore, I'm not travelling in that direction. I shield my eyes to the sunlight and take a step forward, into the future.

Epilogue

"In order to write about life, first you must live it." Ernest Hemingway

Writing this book has been one of the hardest things I have ever done. There will always be the critic that thinks that this is a project for gain. It is. Without a doubt. But not the sort of gain that makes you materially rich. The gains have been emotional and spiritual.

'Karate Doesn't Work In a Phone Box' has been my counsellor, my way of getting all of the stuff that I have never been able to talk about, out. There are parts of this story that evoke so much internal pain. A pain that will never go away. The death of my daughters, the realisation of the poverty my family found ourselves in, the mindless and often brutal violence that blighted my youth and the events that ultimately led to this book, an attempt at taking my own life. Shining a spotlight on mental health is like giving out your bank account details and saying, "Help yourself." You know that it will benefit people, but you also know that it can leave you in a state of ruin. My aim in writing this book was never to glamourise violence, a 'look at how tough I am' journal. It is the opposite. It highlights that acts of aggression make you weak in the long term. The book was written in the different voices we have throughout our life. So, some of the descriptions and justifications are as they would have been to the teenage and early 20's me. We grow in more than just physicality as we age and that is why it sometimes takes us a long time to learn from those that are wise. A real tragedy of life is to continue on the same self-destructive path and never learn. Never change direction. I have been fortunate to have such beautiful family and friends. People that I have at times pushed away, hurt, and turned my back on. But it is a testament to them, that they are still in my life. Refusing to walk away. Able to have seen something in me that I could never see. Our worst prison is the one we build in our mind. It sometimes feels like there is no escape plan, no chance of parole and that we are doomed to end our days locked in solitary confinement. I was that prisoner. In my mind I had committed the worst crimes and deserved my cell. I couldn't see that the bars are not strong enough to hold those that are determined to be free. I do now, or at least I do today. I know that I have a terminal condition. My mind will always be my Achilles heel. But, as Sun Tzu said, "If you know the enemy and know yourself you need not fear the results of a hundred battles."

If this book can help people that are in a similar position to me then all of the battles and struggles I have had in my quest for good mental health will have been worth it. Thanks for reading.

Gary Savage, 2019.